Marketing Methods for Small Factors & Brokers

Tools from the Trenches to Make
Your Factoring Business Thrive!

Jeff Callender

Federal Way, Washington

Marketing Methods for Small Factors & Brokers

Tools from the Trenches to Make Your Factoring Business Thrive!

by Jeff Callender

Published by:
Dash Point Publishing, Inc.
P.O. Box 25591
Federal Way, WA 98093-2591 U.S.A.

Website: www.DashPointPublishing.com

© 2012 by Jeff Callender

A previous edition of this book was published under the title *Marketing Tools for Small Factors and Consultants,* © 2004, 2005, 2006 by Jeff Callender.

All Rights Reserved. No part of this book may be reproduced, stored in a retrieval system, or transmitted in any form or by any means, electronic, mechanical, photocopying, recording, scanning or otherwise, except as expressly permitted by law, without prior written permission of the author, except for the inclusion of brief quotations in a review. Requests for permission should be addressed to Dash Point Publishing, Inc., PO Box 25591, Federal Way, WA 98093-2591.

This publication is designed to provide accurate and authoritative information in regard to the subject mattered covered. It is sold with the understanding that the author and publisher are not engaged in rendering professional services. If professional advice or other expert assistance is required, the services of a competent professional person should be sought.

While every reasonable attempt has been made to obtain accurate information, the author and publisher hereby disclaim any liability for problems due to errors, omissions, or changed information in this publication.

Fictitious names of people and companies are used in this book. Any similarity between these and names of actual people and companies is unintended and purely coincidental.

Library of Congress Control Number: 2012943557

ISBN: 978-1-938837-04-3 (Paperback)
ISBN: 978-1-938837-16-6 (PDF)
ISBN: 978-1-938837-22-7 (Kindle)
ISBN: 978-1-938837-10-4 (ePub)

Printed in the United States of America.

Dedication

Dedicated to those
who contributed to this book,
and the readers who benefit from it.

Contents

PART 1 OVERVIEW 7

Introduction 9
   The Story Behind This Book 9
   The Contributors 11

PART 2 CONTRIBUTORS & THEIR MARKETING METHODS 13

Kim Deveney 15
   Marketing Defined 16
   Top Three Marketing Methods: 16
   Other Marketing Methods to Consider 17
   Marketing Methods to Skip 20
   Marketing Budget – Dollars and Time 20
   Marketing Plan 21
   Advice 22

Melissa Donald 25
   Background 26
   Most Effective Methods 26
   Other Methods 29
   Marketing Budget 30
   Relationship Building 31

Ryan Jaskiewicz 33
   Role of Marketing 34
   Top Three Methods 34
   Marketing Budget 37
   Advice 37

Tony Neglia 39
   Most Effective Methods 40
   Less Effective Methods 41
   Ineffective Methods 41

Anne Gordon 43
   The Role of Marketing in My Broker Business 43
   Advice 44
   Top Marketing Methods 46
   What Somewhat Worked 53
   What Didn't Work 54
   Final Advice 55

RaeLynn Schkade 57
   Background... 58
   Marketing Strategy 59
   Marketing Basics 60
   Less Effective Methods 61
   More Effective Methods....................................... 61
   Summary.. 66
   Advice.. 66
Don D'Ambrosio... 69
   The Need for Marketing 70
   Social Media 70
   Press Releases.. 71
Jeff Callender 75
   Definition of Marketing....................................... 76
   Best Marketing Methods 76
   Somewhat Effective Methods.............................. 84
   Methods That Have Not Worked......................... 87
   Marketing Costs in Dollars and Time................. 88
   Elevator Speech 89
   Advice.. 90

PART 3 ANALYSIS.. 91
Analysis.. 93
   Assessment 93
   Resources Chart 94
   Marketing Methods Chart.................................... 96
   Marketing Methods Analysis............................... 97

CONCLUSION 105
Conclusion 107

APPENDIX 109
Contributors' Information 111
Books and Ebooks.. 112
Acknowledgments.. 119
Important Notice 119
Also by Jeff Callender.. 120
About the Author 121

Part 1

Overview

Introduction

The Story Behind This Book

The best and most effect methods of marketing a small factoring business is one of the first issues facing people who decide to enter this field. Most people without much experience finding new clients often learn by the all-too-familiar "Spaghetti Technique" – throw a lot against the wall and see what sticks.

I addressed the topic of marketing a small factoring business in the chapter "Marketing: How to Find Clients" in the book *How to Run a Small Factoring Business*. Many readers new to the industry have the same questions: "Which marketing methods are most effective?" "Which are a waste of time and money?" "Which should I use?" "Which do *you* use?"

After hearing these questions time and again, the need for this book was obvious. Yet I hesitated writing it because I have never felt marketing to be my strong point as a small factor. I enjoy working with brokers, operations and running the business, and working with clients; but I've never possessed an innate skill in *finding* them. Some people seem to be born marketers, but I'm not one of them.

After the success of the book *Factoring Case Studies*, a joint effort between myself and other small factors (which, to my thinking, is in many ways the most instructive book of The Small Factor Series), I realized a similar approach would provide the most value for a book on marketing. Rather than just telling what marketing methods are being done and what has worked for me, readers could benefit more from learning what works for *several* small factors. So I set out to ask a number of colleagues if they would be willing to contribute to this effort.

Each writer was given the same nine points to address, which were the following:

1. Give a brief definition of marketing and the role it plays in your factoring or factor consulting business.

2. Describe marketing methods you've used and indicate their financial cost and time involved. Separate your responses this way:

    a. The top three marketing methods that work best for you, and why they are successful.

    b. Other marketing methods you recommend which have brought new clients, and why they are worth using.

    c. Methods you have used which aren't as productive, and why they are less beneficial.

    d. Methods which have never worked for you or you will never use again. Explain why you think these methods aren't worthwhile.

3. Discuss approximately how much (in dollars and/or percent of your budget) you spend on marketing per month and per year.

4. Describe approximately how many hours per day, week, and/or month you spend in marketing efforts. If you have a schedule for marketing, tell us what it is.

5. If you have developed a marketing plan, give an outline of its contents and briefly describe your overall strategy.

6. Do you have a standard presentation or "talk," especially the first time you speak with prospects in person or over the phone? If so, please share what you say, and/or look for, in such discussions.

7. What advice would you give to new factors as they search for clients?

8. Discuss any other information about marketing you think is important.

The Contributors

As you will see, each writer answers these questions in his or her own style and from a distinct perspective. While we'll find some overlap as to what has worked and what hasn't, each writer's unique experience is valuable for newcomers to hear, absorb, and apply to their own businesses.

Here are some simple demographics on the writers' backgrounds:

- Four are women, four are men.
- They live in all areas of the country:
  - the Northwest (Washington and Idaho)
  - the West Coast (California - 2)
  - the Midwest (Illinois and Kansas)
  - the Northeast (Rhode Island)
  - the Southeast (Tennessee).
- Seven are full-time small factors. One is a long-time factoring broker who also works for a small factoring company.

In the next section, you will find a picture, bio, and website information about each contributor. These introductory pages about each writer are followed by their responses to the questions outlined above, and describe the various marketing methods each writer uses, has used, and has found unsatisfactory.

Part 3 provides an analysis of the information from the previous section. We'll summarize which methods work the best for the most contributors, which are least effective, and provide this data through charts that make summarizing this material easy to quantify and remember. Part 4 concludes the discussion, and the Appendix provides contributors' names, companies, websites, and locations.

While the subject of marketing is a daunting one, the information in this book provides an excellent starting point for new small factors and brokers who are looking for clients. Those who have been in the business for some time and are looking for new ideas, or want to see how their colleagues tackle this crucial part of the business, will benefit as well. Let's begin!

Marketing Methods for Small Factors & Brokers

Part 2

Contributors & Their Marketing Methods

Marketing Methods for Small Factors & Brokers

Kim Deveney

American Funding Solutions LLC
www.funding4you.com

Blue Springs, Missouri

Kim Deveney is a graduate of the University of Missouri – Columbia, where she received a BS in Accounting. She earned her Master's in Business Administration from Webster University in Kansas City. She worked as an accountant for State Street for eleven years before starting American Funding Solutions LLC in August of 2003 in Blue Springs, Missouri.

As managing partner she has helped numerous small businesses improve their cash flow with factoring. American Funding specializes in small ticket factoring transactions of services to various industries except construction and third party medical factoring. Kim has a passion for helping small businesses and is a proud member of the International Factoring Association. She is a founding member of The Factoring Alliance LLC which helps to educate and promote factoring to the small business community.

Marketing Defined

Marketing is the process of telling potential clients about your business and how you can help solve their problems. Marketing is important in any business, including the factoring industry. Marketing is often more challenging in the factoring industry because many business owners are unaware of the concept. It can be a challenge to help them understand factoring, how it works, and how it can benefit their business.

I have found the best way to market factoring is by sharing examples of how you have helped businesses become more successful and improve their cash flow. Share a story of a specific company, and explain how cash flow shortage was hindering their growth. Explain how your business was able to provide immediate access to cash using only their invoices. A story can be a powerful example of how factoring works and can benefit small businesses.

Top Three Marketing Methods:

Become the Expert. Write articles for your local business journal, give seminars to SBDC (Small Business Development Centers), EDC's (Economic Development Corps), business groups, chambers, etc. Prepare a "Lunch & Learn" for local bankers or accountants to educate them on the factoring process and how it may be helpful to their small business clients. Become known as the "expert" in your community for providing alternative forms of funding for small businesses.

Post informational articles on your blog, LinkedIn, and other social media venues. Look for questions about cash flow and small business financing on various social media sites and respond to these questions with educational information about factoring, being careful not to be seen as "trying to sell" your service. The key is to share information and not sell your services.

Subscribe to RSS feeds to get daily or weekly links related to small businesses or factoring topics. This is a great way to use your social media venues, and find questions or topics to which you can respond in order to enhance your "expert" status.

Referral Groups. Find a referral group (sometimes called a "leads group") in your local area. The fee to join a referral group can range from $125 to $700 per year. I have been a member of groups that were very expensive and some that were free. In my opinion, the more expensive groups are not necessarily better, just more formal and have more structure. The most important aspect of any referral group is the members. Try to find a group that includes a small business banker, accountant, lawyer, financial planner, and others that will be good referral sources for your factoring business.

It may take time to find the right group because many groups will include industries that are not a complementary referral source for factoring (i.e. multi-level marketers, realtors, mortgage professionals, home based businesses, etc.) Although anyone can provide a referral occasionally, you should strive to find a group that is made up of a few people that could refer business to you on a regular basis.

Brokers. Work with a broker and spend the time to educate him/her on the exact type of transactions you are looking to factor. Make sure the broker knows your niche market and thoroughly understand factoring and how it can benefit small businesses. The broker should be able to properly explain the factoring process and related benefits to prospects. In addition, ensure the broker knows the types of industries you will not factor and help them find other sources for those types of transactions.

Other Marketing Methods to Consider

Chambers. Join and become active in your local chamber of commerce. The chamber is an excellent way to meet other business owners and referral sources. I have not found a significant amount of businesses that need factoring services within my chamber, but I have found numerous referral sources. As a member, you obtain a copy of the Membership Directory. The directory is filled with numerous bankers, accountants, financial planners, etc. who are excellent referral partners.

As a member, I made appointments with each of these referral partners to get to know them better and discuss how we can be referral sources for each other. Without exception, every person I called was open and receptive to getting together for coffee or lunch because I was a member and we both specialize in working with small business owners. They could see the benefit of aligning our resources to better serve our small business clients.

The best way to make your chamber experience beneficial is to get involved. The other chamber members need to see you active and involved. This will help you begin to build relationship with the various members who are your new referral sources. Join a committee, or volunteer for a leadership position within the chamber to get the most out of your membership.

The cost of a chamber membership can vary from $100 to $1000 depending on how large your city is and how many members the chamber has. The larger chambers are often more expensive, although many chambers charge a lower price for their small business members verses corporate members. Other chambers have pricing related to the number of employees of the business which could also be advantageous for small businesses with minimal employees.

Business Groups. Consider joining other business groups where you will begin to build relationships with other small business owners, referral sources, or businesses in a specific target industry. Some of these groups could include, NAWBO (National Association of Women Business Owners), NARI (National Association of the Remodeling Industry), Toastmasters, American Club Association, construction associations, staffing associations, etc.

Find a group whose meetings you enjoy attending and get involved. Many of these groups have monthly meetings with keynote speakers. The meetings will help you become a better business owner while introducing you to other businesses and referral partners.

Cold Calls. I started my business doing all cold calls. I found free business lists using Reference USA from my local library. This process is inexpensive but very time consuming. You must make numerous calls each day, have a tracking system for follow up, and withstand a lot of rejection.

I did get my first few clients using this method but I would not recommend it to others. The sales process is long and very unsatisfying. Often you are educating the prospect about factoring, only to have them start researching other companies and begin rate shopping. As a broker, I spent weeks working with one business owner, only to lose the client to another factoring company for a 1/4 point difference in fees.

Typically, when you use this method the prospect doesn't feel any loyalty to you and closing a deal it is very hard. I would only suggest this form of marketing to someone new in the industry who wants to "practice" explaining factoring and its benefits to a prospect. This type of marketing will definitely help you get your "30 second elevator speech" perfected and you may get a client or two in the process.

Pay Per Click. Pay per click internet marketing can be a successful method if you have a large marketing budget. I hired a firm to help find the best keywords and develop marketing campaigns around those keywords. I had a budget of $1,000 per month based on keywords related to factoring. Prospects were directed to my website to complete a very short contact form requesting more information.

I soon realized that my $1,000 monthly budget was not adequate to generate sufficient leads using the pay per click method. I received 3-5 contact forms per week but only closed one new client in 15 months of using this method. I found that prospects that completed the contact form, had also completed contact forms from several other factoring companies. When I would call back, the prospect would say, "Hmm...which company are you with?" Most of the prospects were "internet shopping" or just wanting to get information about factoring. I do know of other factors with much larger monthly budgets who seem to have much more success with this method.

Advertising. Advertise in specific trade journals or small business newspapers or magazines. For example, if your target marketing is the staffing industry, place an advertisement in a journal that caters to the staffing industry.

In your advertisement ensure you are addressing the problem or the "pain" that staffing companies often encounter, and then solve their problem with factoring. For example, the advertisement might say,

"All successful staffing businesses occasionally struggle with cash flow. Factoring can provide immediate access to working capital for increased payroll demands."

Also consider advertising in areas where small businesses often frequent. For example, a golf course, small business enterprise center, coffee shop, or local café.

Advertising can be cost prohibitive for a new business. I would not suggest advertising as your main form of marketing. Instead I would suggest advertising only as another method if your marketing budget allows for the additional expense. If not, there are lots of less expensive ways to market your business.

Marketing Methods to Skip

Direct Mail. Direct mail has not proved successful for my business. I tried direct mail a few years ago without any success. The lists can be expensive to purchase and many of the addresses are outdated so the mail is returned. Today with social media, increased postage rates, and an overabundance of junk mail, I would strongly discourage anyone from using direct mail. The process is time consuming and expensive with minimal results.

Marketing Budget – Dollars and Time

My marketing budget is minimal. I spend approximately $100 per month attending networking events, chamber events, and other marketing efforts. In addition, my budget includes approximately $3,000 in annual membership dues for the chamber, NAWBO, IFA, my leads group, etc. The annual membership dues are collected once a year typically on the anniversary of your membership. Therefore, the annual marketing budget ranges from $4,500-$5,000 per year.

I spend an average of 7-10 hours per week on my marketing efforts. These hours are spent attending networking events with the chamber, attending weekly meetings with my leads group, and making phone calls derived from these efforts. I also spend time following up on previous referrals and leads who I have not been able to reach or have requested call backs.

I send monthly emails to my referral partners using Constant Contact to stay in front of them. I share success stories of small businesses we have helped with our factoring services. I set up coffee or lunch meetings with existing and new referral sources to continue to build relationships.

Every Friday I plan my upcoming week, being sure to include two to three networking events, time to follow-up on referrals, and time to meet with my referral sources.

Marketing Plan

My marketing plan consists of three main strategies:

1. Brokers
2. Networking for referral partners
3. Social media.

1. Brokers

The marketing plan consists of working closely with my brokers to find small businesses in need of factoring services. I spend time educating my brokers on the specific type of businesses we can help and explain the reasons we cannot help other type of businesses. I help the brokers understand our due diligence process and work with them to pre-screen referrals to prevent wasting time on non-doable transactions.

2. Networking for Referral Partners

In my networking efforts, I try to search out referral partners verses looking for small businesses that might need factoring services. For example, when I go to a Chamber of Commerce luncheon, I will try to network with bankers or accountants who could be a good referral on an ongoing basis. It is a better use of my time to network for referral partners as compared to using the networking time to find businesses that need factoring.

Once I have made a connection with a banker, attorney, or accountant that could be an ongoing referral partner, I make an effort to continue to build that relationship. I will take them to lunch to get to know them better. I will drop them a note or card occasionally to help them remember me and how we help small businesses.

3. Social Media

I use social media to help be seen as the "expert" in my industry. I blog about small business topics, use Twitter to share articles that could be beneficial to small businesses, and use LinkedIn to post articles and factoring information. I have joined groups within LinkedIn that include small business owners. Within these groups, I try to answer questions posed by group members related to financing or cash flow to further explain factoring and how it may be a valuable financing option for small business.

I use Constant Contact to stay in touch with my referral partners and clients. I will send a note monthly about a financing topic. I will also share recent success stories related to factoring and my small business clients.

My marketing goal with regard to social media is not to sell factoring services, but instead to educate people on financing options and other small business tips. I use social medial as a way to stay in front of my referral partners and be seen as an "expert" within the industry. Social media is an excellent tool, but one should be careful not to bombard your contacts with too many posts, e-mails, etc. My marketing plan includes weekly blogs, tweets, and updates to Facebook and LinkedIn. Social media is great way to "touch" your referral partners and clients on a periodic basis.

Advice

As a new factor or consultant in the industry, decide which of the many marketing methods you will employ. Think about your strengths and weaknesses, and take into to consideration your marketing budget. Decide which marketing methods will be best suited for your personality. Pick three marketing methods and stick with them for a minimum of six months before deciding if the method is working for you. Remember you may need to get outside of your comfort zone on occasion to meet new people to develop your referral sources but it will be well worth your efforts. After experimenting with your top three marketing methods for six months re-evaluate and make changes if necessary.

In addition, you will need to become proficient at explaining your business using a 30 second "elevator speech." Develop a speech you can easily recite to help people understand your business. For example my elevator speech is, "Hello, I specialize in working with small businesses and help them improve their cash flow using their invoices. We try to be another option for small businesses that want to obtain working capital without incurring additional debt. Our funding program is extremely simple and flexible and can often provide funds to small business even when their bank cannot provide assistance."

Marketing is extremely important and it can often get overlooked as you get busy with your factoring business. This is especially true if you are factoring clients directly rather than being a broker. Regardless of how busy you may find yourself, you should always make time for marketing and networking with your referral sources. It will help to keep your referral "pipeline" full. I have seen several small businesses get "too busy to market" and they often find themselves without clients after several months of neglecting their marketing efforts. Continuous marketing efforts are extremely important to the success of your business!

Marketing Methods for Small Factors & Brokers

Melissa Donald

LDI Growth Partners
www.ldifactors.com

Walnut Creek, California

Melissa Donald spent the first eleven years of her career working in and then managing a commercial collection agency. In 2001, she left the collection industry and took a position with a factoring firm in Walnut Creek, California. During her tenure, Melissa worked her way from a Senior Account Executive to Operations Manager to Vice President of Operations.

In January 2007, Melissa and her two partners launched LDI Growth Partners. LDI works diligently and intentionally to increase awareness of the benefits of factoring for businesses in all stages of growth, and to work side by side with clients to create tailored factoring programs that fit their unique needs.

LDI Growth Partners works with clients in all stages of growth, and focusses on businesses in the early stages, generally from start up to about $1M-$2M in annual sales. While not industry specific, LDI works with many contractors and trades people who are working with banks and real estate brokers to rehab homes after foreclosure. LDI's portfolio includes businesses of all types, from the neighborhood florist (account debtors are funerals homes) to cutting edge technology companies who are using factoring to bide time and increase the valuation of their company before taking on venture capital.

Marketing Methods for Small Factors & Brokers

Background

I have been in the factoring industry since 2001. I started in Operations and never considered that I would be the driving force for marketing and sales in any company, let alone my own. As an Ops person, I had a tension-filled relationship with the sales people and brokers in the company for whom I worked; frankly, Operations made a whole lot more sense to me than all of that fluffy, salesy stuff.

The irony is not lost on me that I now spend roughly half my time in some sort of sales capacity, working to build new referral relationships, maintaining and strengthening existing ones and continually refining our target market.

LDI Growth Partners is not a niche factor. We do not focus on a specific industry or size deal. We made the decision when we started the company in 2007 that we would only do deals that "make sense" to us. As a result, we have a varied portfolio, from the neighborhood florist to cutting edge technology companies with AAA+ account debtors. If I had to pick a "sweet spot" – the ideal client – it would be a business doing between $500K-2M in annual sales and whose account debtors are strong regional credits.

Most Effective Methods

It truly was a fluke that I ended up learning how to network and sell. I made a promise (to my then boss/investor) that I would figure out how to bring in business. Two days later, at a dinner at my church, one of my friends told me about this little networking group he belonged to called BNI, Business Network International (www.bni.com). He told me that there could only be one person per profession in the group and there was already a "finance" person. I laughed and told him, "Not my kind of finance!" That was in December 2005.

Shortly after I received and closed my first referral as a BNI member I attended a sales and marketing class for factors. One of the moderators stood up in front of the room and announced "Don't ever bother with those breakfast networking meetings; you will never receive any quality business." I wanted to slide off my chair, under the table, and hide. "Holy cow," I thought, "I am doing this all wrong." I walked away from that class pretty sure that I needed to go flip burgers somewhere.

In hindsight, I am still not sure why we made the decision to stick to how we were doing things. I just knew that it made sense to me and I have never been afraid to fly in the face of conventional wisdom.

At the end of 2006, having moderate success with my networking efforts, my then co-worker and I were given the opportunity to go out on our own and start LDI. Those next few months were a flurry of activity when we had to decide exactly what kind of factors we wanted to be. The business model we decided on was a *direct result* of how I liked to network and market the product – from a position of education rather than sales.

I network at the grassroots entrepreneurial level. The first time I did a presentation on factoring I asked the 30 people in the room if they had ever heard of factoring – no one raised their hand. Three years later, I was introduced as a presenter to a room of 200+. The room was asked how many people knew what factoring is. Two-thirds of the people raised their hands!

Once we decided that we were only going to do business locally (all clients are within a two-hour drive of my house), this type of networking and relationship building seemed to really fit the way we wanted to do business. Through my membership in BNI and affiliation with The Referral Institute, I learned how to hone in on what our target market really is *and* how to let my referral partners know what kind of clients we are looking for.

After I had been a member for two years, I applied for and became a Director Consultant for the San Francisco Bay Region of BNI. This position has enabled me to work with business owners all over the Bay Area as a networking expert, rather than just a factoring expert. In fact, I do not "push" factoring or LDI. Discussion of the benefits of factoring comes naturally in conversations and presentations.

Public Speaking/Presentations/Workshops. This is one of my favorite ways to market. I thoroughly enjoy watching the light bulb flicker on when the concept of factoring sinks in. I have spoken and/or participated in panel discussions for almost all of the Chambers of Commerce in my target area. I have presented at workshops for BNI where factoring is not a topic of discussion. I have also spoken at service groups, non-profits and networking groups.

Over time, I have prepared and generated a dozen or so presentations, ranging from 10 minutes to an hour. I test and perfect new material at my BNI meetings and depend on that group of professionals to help me determine if the information I think is pertinent actually matters to other business owners. There have been times when I have realized a couple of minutes into a presentation that the great idea I had planned to talk about (some aspect of factoring) simply did not matter to anyone but me.

One of the other benefits of my affiliation and membership in BNI is from a risk mitigation standpoint. Over time, I have been able to build a team of professionals who all share the team approach to working with our clients, which in turn helps to mitigate risk, and that in turn opens up the marketing possibilities. We are able to take on more eclectic deals because we have a better handle on the overall health and well-being of the client.

We recently signed a client who was turned down by another local factor. I met with the business owner and he walked me through how his business works. I completely understood why the other factor turned the deal away. If I were in their position, I would have done the same. Yet I signed the deal. Why?

Because we had something the other factor didn't have... the super-secret weapon, if you will. I have had breakfast with his older sister every Friday morning for the last four years. I *know* that my new client will not do anything that will cause his sister to be embarrassed or upset. Of every factoring deal we have ever done, that is the *best* risk mitigation I have ever experienced.

Good will. One of the most counter intuitive marketing tools I have found is in the deals we don't do. We have turned down deals that would have been financially lucrative because it did not make sense to do them. This can happen for many reasons.

I recently received a referral from another factor for a take-out (we take over the relationship). In talking with the prospect, it became clear to me that he had a pretty good chance of qualifying for a small personal line of credit with a bank. (Keeping a finger on the pulse of what the banks are able to do is critical.) I told him we would factor his paper during the transition, but I do not anticipate his needing to factor with us for more than three to six months. In that meeting, I referred him to a banker (his loan is in underwriting as I write this), a payroll company, and a bookkeeper who specializes in his industry.

The question is...how does this spin into a marketing friendly situation for LDI? Quite simply, the prospect is so beyond thrilled that I am willing to help him when it costs him nothing. At the same time, I have been able to give referrals to several of my "team" members. Over time, this prospect is going to tell his colleagues about the positive experience he had with LDI and LDI will remain at the forefront of my referral partners' minds.

Other Methods

Over the years, we have tried other methods of marketing, with mixed and varied results:

Print Advertising. We have paid for print advertising in local publications. To my knowledge, we have never booked a client as a result of those efforts. That said, we do continue to do something at least once a year for brand recognition and to keep our name and logo out there. Over time, we have also found that there is a "quid pro quo" in the print advertising world, so generally, any print advertising we do is in conjunction with some sort of article about LDI or in a specifically targeted issue of the publication (focusing on finance, money, growth, etc.).

Brokers/Salespeople. Again, this is a mixed result. We do have a BDO (Business Development Officer), who brings us some deals. He brokers out what we cannot or don't want to do. We do not have, nor do we want, a broker network.

Web Presence. Much to our website designers' chagrin, we do NOT want to drive business through our website, nor do we want to be on page one of a Google search. Because we have built a marketing model that relies almost entirely on personal referral, we would not consider doing business with someone who found us on the internet. It has become my philosophy that if you find us on the internet, you have been turned down by people with a lot more experience than we have.

Social Media. I know that many businesses are starting to rely on the ability of social media to drive business. Again, because of how we have opted to market, we do not look to social media to bring in business. Instead, much like our website, we use social media (Facebook and LinkedIn) as a way to educate about factoring in order to augment our face-to-face marketing efforts.

Other Factors. I resisted this one for a long time. However, as I met with and networked with other small factors, I have found that this tight-knit group of people is each other's best resource. I have also worked with a couple larger factors who need a place to send small deals they come across.

Marketing Budget

As the economy tanked in 2008 and 2009, I was stunned and saddened to find one of the first areas that business owners were cutting in their budget was in marketing and advertising. It was at that time that we increased our budget. It was at that time that I expanded my reach in BNI by becoming a Director Consultant. It was then that I really ramped up speaking and presentations and became more involved in the International Factoring Association (IFA).

Even with the increases, our Marketing budget remains fairly small, less than 3% of our overhead. It is more challenging to quantify the time expense. As best we can determine, my time is split about equally between marketing, risk and relationship management. There is a lot of overlap between these segments, largely because of the holistic approach we take to working with our clients and referral sources.

Relationship Building

When I talk to other factors, both large and small, one of the main themes I hear from a sales perspective is that clients are constantly churning and that they have to continually keep their pipeline full. We have the opposite problem.

Largely, I believe, because of the way we build relationships with our clients and their businesses, our challenge is convincing clients they are ready to move on from us to a more traditional and often much less expensive form of financing. I am working with a client right now to transition them out of our factoring program and into a combination of working capital line of credit with a bank and personal equity line of credit on an inherited property.

We are in the final stages of the process and this is an excerpt from an email I received from them:

> "We are children who don't want to break the strings too soon or get away from our security blanket. We always know you are looking out for our best interest."

This company was with another factor for several years before joining us and had come to believe factoring was going to be part of their business plan forever. We have been working together for almost two years. During that time, the principals have cleaned up their personal credit, hired the right people to help them with the infrastructure of the business, and outsourced services to experts. It is a win/win for all of us as this client has referred others to us and will continue to do so long after they have moved on from us.

I believe the same things that make small factors successful can also be our downfall, and it all starts in how we market. One of the advantages of working with a small factor is clients get hands on, personal attention, often from the owner or principal of the firm. Small factors rely more on instinct than on the paper.

Most of us do not do an in depth financial analysis of our clients information. We each have our hot buttons and things we look for in a deal and we market either to or around those buttons. In truth, as entrepreneurial factors who wear all the hats of the business at one time or another during each day, we cannot practice the "pasta at the wall" method of marketing. In my opinion, we have to spend our marketing time teaching a few key people how to best refer business to us.

I have half a dozen key referral partners. I know when they send something to me, there is better than an 80% chance we will close the deal as it is already been vetted according to our criteria.

Ryan Jaskiewicz

12five Capital, LLC
www.12five.com

Oakbrook Terrace, Illinois

Ryan Jaskiewicz is CEO of 12five Capital, LLC. He graduated from University of Illinois at Chicago with a Bachelor of Arts in Political Science with an emphasis on international politics and economic policy. He grew up with factoring as his father is a 25-plus year veteran of the industry. Ryan recognized his entrepreneurial drive early, and taking the knowledge he learned from his father, started his own factoring firm in early 2006 at the age of 23.

12five provides working capital to small and medium size businesses. It specializes in high growth companies with annual revenues between $100k and $10m. Its goal is to provide financing that is simple, easy, and straightforward to clients, so they can truly understand where their company is positioned and what it will take to grow.

Ryan is married and lives in Riverside, Illinois. When he's not factoring, you can probably find him running the Salt Creek trail, as running marathons is his other love, next to his wife.

Role of Marketing

Marketing for 12five Capital is very important to our business. It is what drives us and keeps the engine running. We believe that marketing has a very wide net. In fact, a goal of ours has always been to be marketing in everything we do. This obviously starts in business development, but can be done in operations, as well.

Top Three Methods

The top three methods of marketing we use are:

1. Networking
2. Social Media
3. Education.

1. Networking. We consider this to be the most important marketing method. Networking is the life blood of a small factoring company, as we do not have the huge marketing budget of a larger firm. We consider networking to be face to face time with individuals that have access to the deal flow that a factoring company needs.

There is a wide group of individuals who have access to rospective clients. The main few we focus on are bankers, CPAs, and turnaround consultants. Bankers are a great source for multiple reasons. They are directly interacting with clients of theirs who are looking for financing. They also understand the highlights or struggles of that client, and can help prequalify a referred prospect.

One of the issues we run into with brokers are those who simply send you everything they find, without learning if they are qualified for factoring. If you have networked and educated your bankers, they should recognize a business that is a good prospect. They are also seeing clients they no longer want to finance for one reason or another. While these bank "rejects" may seem like a red flag, these prospects can often be stronger than those referred from brokers and others.

CPAs are very similar to bankers in that they have tremendous access to their clients' businesses. They are seeing actual numbers on a monthly or quarterly basis. They are also quite adept at understanding cash flow needs, which is a great asset to have in our business. Getting to know a group of close CPAs can pay off dividends in the form of steady deal flow for years to come. The key is creating a lasting working relationship. Without it, they'll simply go to the next person on the list.

Turnaround consultants are another great source of prospective clients, albeit the deals are generally larger than the average small factor can support. That said, if you are a smaller to medium size factor or have a great deal of funds to put to work, this can be a great referral source. These consultants are brought in by banks and investors to turnaround the business client they have. Often times, these clients are struggling with cash flow issues. These turnaround consultants generally don't have resources of their own to finance these companies, so they need to look to other sources for the financing. This is where a factoring company can provide assistance in the turnaround of a business, as well as growing their own company through acquisition of clients like these. Again, creating long lasting relationships is vital, as you want to be first on the list for these sources.

Outstanding Customer Service. At 12five, we believe we have an opportunity to market in every aspect of our business, including day-to-day operations. This includes providing outstanding personal service to our clients as well to our clients' customers. Having the best customer service is a primary focus of our business. It is essentially free marketing for the business. We have had multiple word of mouth referrals from current clients to prospects in the same field. This is beneficial since we are already familiar with the ins and outs of the business in which they work. It also gives the prospect a sense of comfort, since we were referred by a friend or colleague. Anytime you can start a business relationship on a comfortable note, the better.

2. Social Media. Speaking of "friends" and colleagues, we also market on social media pretty heavily. By this I don't mean "spamming" Twitter and Facebook. Rather, we believe that it is important to build an audience that cares about what you have to say. This can be anyone, from friends to clients to industry associates.

We understand this is a relatively new form of marketing, and feel it is a medium that cannot be ignored. We believe that by posting relevant content and interacting with our followers, we are creating a base for all different types of business. Relevant content could be anything from posting articles and information about industry trends, to updating our Facebook page or running Facebook ads.

Facebook. On Facebook there are many different ways to approach marketing. First and foremost, we feel it is important for us to set up a Facebook page for our company where we present our company to Facebook users. While many people assume that this may be a waste of time due to a perceived demographic, they couldn't be farther from the truth.

In fact, the demographics are interesting. 49% of all users are between the ages of 26 - 54. In the United States alone, there are just over 70 million users between the ages of 26-54. This is a number that we choose not to ignore. Currently, over 30% of our website traffic comes from Facebook alone.

We also employ the use of Facebook ads. Facebook ads allow for great analysis and detail when you are creating an ad campaign. They allow for you to whittle down to an exact market that you want to choose and they will give you the exact number of users to whom you will be advertising. For example, you may choose the 25-54 age demographic, or filter it to show your ad only to men, or only to people interested in entrepreneurship. Again, this allows the marketing campaign to be tailored to each factoring company's particular needs.

Twitter. We use Twitter in a way similar to that of Facebook. We have a company Twitter account, which primarily posts updates about the company, specials we may be running, events in which we may be involved, speaking engagements, photos, etc. We also like to quote articles or news that may be of interest to our clients and colleagues.

The whole point is to build an audience that wants to hear what you have to say. It is also about branding both yourself and your company, in a way that personalizes the business.

This may not be the goal for every company, which is fine. However, if it is the goal of a company to become more socially involved, then Facebook and Twitter are the obvious first steps in that direction.

Marketing Budget

As a small business, we spend probably around $5,000-$10,000 a year on marketing efforts. This can be from meals and entertainment for referral sources, to Facebook and Google ads.

We have a dedicated managing director whose main objective is business development. This means we spend roughly 50-60 hours per week on marketing.

We choose not to have a set marketing "talk" that we give because we feel that makes things sound scripted. We believe in what we do, and that belief allows us to market and sell our service in a sincere and productive way. We listen to all the questions and understand the needs of most clients. By not scripting our conversations, it allows us to be genuine with our clients and listen in a way that provides them the best possible factoring program for their company.

Advice

My advice for new factors trying to crack into the industry this: you need to "pound the pavement." There is nothing better for procuring prospects than getting your face in front of the bankers, CPAs, and attorneys that have access to these leads. For us, taking the approach of the long term relationship with these sources is the only way to build a sustainable book of factoring business.

Marketing Methods for Small Factors & Brokers

Tony Neglia

Stonebridge Financial Services, Inc.
www.stonebridgefs.com

Brentwood, Tennessee

Tony Neglia graduated from the University of Pennsylvania in 1986 with a bachelor's degree in mathematics. He started his career as an actuary in Philadelphia, and his job took him to New York, Paris, Japan, Australia and London. After twenty years in the actuarial field, Tony settled in Brentwood, Tennessee in 2004 where he currently resides.

Tony began as a factor in 2006, starting Stonebridge Financial Services. He specializes in factoring small companies and will purchase invoices as low as $200, with volume as high as $50,000 per month with most industries, with the exception of construction, third party medical and trucking. Tony is active in the factoring community and is has served on the Board of Directors of the International Factoring Association.

When he is not busy servicing Stonebridge clients he can be found at the Nashville Chess Center where he serves on the Board of Directors as its Treasurer. He also volunteers at local schools promoting and teaching chess to children of all ages in the Nashville area.

Most Effective Methods

Brokers. When our business started, we were lucky enough to be introduced to brokers in the cash flow business. To this day most of our leads (and consequently most of our business) come from brokers.

Our brokers are (almost) worth their weight in gold and we treat them with kid gloves. We follow up on leads immediately and give updates back to our brokers as to where things stand and if necessary, why we can't fund a deal. We pay commissions on the first or the second of every month without fail in the hope that we are the first commission payment they receive every month. We want them to know that we value them.

Other Factors. We attend two out of state meetings a year (usually the annual IFA conference in the spring and an IFA workshop in the fall). While these meetings are informative and keep us abreast of changes in the industry, I have also found them very good networking opportunities! There are many opportunities to network with

1. large factoring companies looking for a home for their unwanted leads
2. small factoring companies looking for participants or funding sources
3. companies who have expertise in areas about which you may be thinking.

I always carry business cards with me and when appropriate, hand them out and explain how factoring works.

Over time we have built relationships with larger factoring companies (some of whom we met at IFA meetings) who send us leads that are too small for them. We have quite a few clients who have come to us this way. In turn, if we get a lead that is too big for us we try to return the favor and send leads back to them. Of course, since most of our leads come from independent brokers we don't own them. As a result, if a broker lead is too large we cannot send it to another factoring company without permission from the broker.

Clients. We pay referral fees to our clients when they send a lead (that becomes a client) our way. This is a great source of leads and we have a few clients who came to us this way. Additionally, since your client referred them to you they are, in a sense, pre-qualified. Your client probably doesn't want to send you bad leads. Also, they likely have similar (or the same) customers as your client so you already know how well they pay.

Less Effective Methods

Local Branch Bankers. Over the years I have gotten to know the bankers at our local branch quite well. I always take a little time to explain to them what factoring is and I rarely miss an opportunity to bring them a gift for Christmas, New Year's, birthdays, etc. This mild form of bribery has worked well and every once in a while we get a lead from them. When the leads slow down I look for another excuse to bring them some chocolates or a new mug, etc. My goal is to keep them thinking of us when they have a client who is declined a loan – of which there are many.

Website. I have not focused on internet marketing for a number of reasons, the primary reason being I have no expertise in this area. I view my website as an online brochure rather than a means of generating leads. A website is very important and lends credibility to your business but unless it is designed as a sales tool it shouldn't be used as such. There is a glut of companies out there who specialize in website design and that can help you set up a well-designed page. Tread carefully however, it can be very expensive and unless you know how to drive leads to your website cheaply you can spend a lot of money with very little return. We leave this to others.

Ineffective Methods

Leads Groups. The first year I spent a great deal of time pursuing local networking opportunities (i.e. BNI meetings, chambers of commerce, etc.). As a one person business it was difficult attending so many meetings as well as servicing the leads we were getting from brokers (to say nothing of running the day to day transactions of the business). After about a year our local networking efforts yielded very few results. It was an easy decision to focus on the leads I was getting from brokers.

Other Bankers and Accountants. We have contacted bankers, accountants, etc. and very little has come from it.

Print Advertisements. We also did print advertisements in a (now closed) cash flow journal for a couple years. We got a few calls from people thinking about getting into the brokering business but that was it. I didn't build any long term relationships with brokers and didn't get any deals. I have considered advertising in a local business journal but have not pulled the trigger due to the cost.

Anne Gordon

Guilin Group, Inc.
www.guilinfunding.com

Wickford, Rhode Island

Anne Gordon was born in Hackensack, NJ and grew up in Wickford, Rhode Island. She graduated from Simmons College in Boston with a Bachelor's degree in Marketing. She then went to work at Orhbach's department store in New York City for three years as an assistant buyer. She then worked for May Company, importing merchandise from Europe. This was followed by working as a corporate buyer for JC Penney for 23 years, purchasing merchandise from the Far East. She became aware of factoring while working at JC Penney, and also earned her MBA in Marketing at New York University School of Business Administration while employed at JC Penney.

Anne and her husband Gene Spaulding started Guilin Group Inc. in 1995 and worked on real estate investments until 2002, when they started brokering factoring deals. The two worked the business until Gene's passing in 2011. Anne has continued the business on her own since then. Rather than a direct funder, Anne has always worked in the factoring field as a broker. She also works with Dash Point Financial, where she is responsible for following up with slow paying accounts as well as screening prospective new clients. Her years of business experience plus her depth of factoring knowledge is a great asset to the company.

The Role of Marketing in My Broker Business

Marketing is 85-90% of my brokering business. It's not one, but many activities, but first and foremost prospects must have confidence and trust in you as a factoring professional. I make a concentrated effort to make the prospect feel at ease talking with me. I am dealing with their livelihood, and the survival of their business in many cases. Relationship building is the most important part of the marketing process. I make every effort to be approachable, a good listener and note taker, and empathetic to the personal side as well as the business side of my prospects' worlds.

So while I describe what works and does not work for me, it has always been intertwined with my personality. Marketing and my business have to be in accord with my own comfort zone.

Advice

Remember, no matter what you do or who you are, when you are involved in marketing you are in sales. No matter how wonderful your website, how spectacular your brochure, or how glossy your business card, the ultimate success of your business is your relationships and how you handle them. These are relatively easy across a table with a cup of coffee, but in today's world, the challenge is to establish them and keep them going over the phone, in emails, and through the internet.

Be passionate about what you do, and realize most people do not understand factoring. You must be involved, understand the business, and be ready to work with the fear your prospect may have about using financing that is not from a bank. Traditional financial institutions are not as accessible to regular businesses as they once were. Although factoring has been around for centuries, the majority of business people still have not heard of it.

Because I am a broker rather than a direct lender, many times I am asked where the money comes from; some think it is from the mysterious "underground." When I first joined Women's Business Council, one of the board members did not want to approve my membership because she thought I was either a loan shark or using "laundered money." She had never heard of factoring. Grudgingly, she gave in after I explained that some banks offer this service, in addition to a great number of factoring companies of all sizes.

Be willing to give your time, your attention, your knowledge, and all your effort as you establish the relationship with a prospect. Share events where the prospect can network to get more business. Being a Certified WBE (Women's Business Enterprise) I am on every request for bid list, networking buyer/seller event, and trade show list I can be. I share the information, contacts, and project listings I get from these resources with prospective clients to help them get more work and make valuable contacts. It costs you little time and effort to forward these emails or fax copies with a note on the front. Make every effort to personalize these emails and faxes. Again, make the prospect feel valued; their success is your success. Whether this person has become your client or not, nurture that relationship. You don't know whom they know and can refer to you, whether they use your service or not.

Be a good listener. When a client is describing his/her business needs, this is the time to *be quiet*. Just listen and take notes. By listening and asking questions, you are "selling yourself" in a very subtle but productive way. Your attitude, your body language, your responses are what project the trust and strength that your prospect needs.

You are helping them save face. Remember, chances are they have been to several other places looking for funding, and in many cases rejected by all of them. Although they know they need money, they are not aware of exactly how to get it. You may be their only hope. Many times have I been told they were waiting to hear from an investor or asked if I know any venture capitalists, but they have no idea of the requirements of these sources of funds. All they see is the end result, which is fueled by their need for money.

Do not promise more than you can deliver. Especially when you are first starting out, you just know you can solve everyone's financing problems. Not true. This perception is a waste of your time – and the prospect's. Educate yourself as to what works and what doesn't. Read the other books by Jeff Callender to start your education.

If a prospect does not fit into the parameters of factoring, don't lead him on. As difficult as it may be sometimes, tell the truth, and do it sooner rather than later. Both of you will be better for it. However, if you find an option for this prospect, go back and say, "Do you still need financing? I was talking to another funding source who might have a solution for you, and decided to give you a call. Do you think this program will work for you?' Again, continue to strengthen the relationship.

"Mess up – fess up. An old saying, but a basic one. We all make mistakes and humility is endearing. It establishes or strengthens trust.

Top Marketing Methods

Networking Groups. Chambers of commerce and networking groups were our first marketing efforts, and they were modestly successful. We targeted the banks at all events.

Factoring is not a word that is on everyone's lips, like insurance. Banking people at networking groups are looking for new customers, not alternative funding sources. We would take their card, introduce ourselves, and then call or email later to arrange to sit down in the bank with them to go over how we could help. Trust me, this was an incredible education for most of them. They were clueless about factoring, but they listened. Those who knew about it believed all they needed was one factor.

However, we explained each factoring company has a niche and its own qualifications and requirements. We also emphasized the benefit to the bank: they could keep the deposits and continued relationship with the customer. When the customer was bankable, the door was wide open at the bank. When banks came on board with us, they would call us their Capital Affiliate or something equally impressive. Once again, relationship building became the foundation for referrals from the banks. I still get calls and emails to help their customers.

We continued the networking groups for a couple years, building and solidifying the banking relationships. We always kept a scorecard of where the leads came from. Every 4-6 months, we would look over where the activity was coming from, drop memberships, or investigate new ones.

Believe me, when you are doing as many as three networking events a day – breakfast, lunch, then after hours – you are tired! You need to really focus on which ones are productive. Gene and I did not always go together; depending on the size of the organization, we would cover two different breakfasts or after hours events. Then constantly and quickly following each event, sending follow-up emails and making calls for appointments were crucial. It is very important to follow-up, but to also keep track of progress.

The one group I still belong to is Women's Business Council. Guilin Group Inc. is a Certified Woman Owned Enterprise. This is a national certification, and as a result, government contracting officers and procurement officers refer companies to me. As a WBE, my company falls under one of the government set aside programs. Although I do not bid on any contracts, I use this certification as a marketing tool.

When you belong to a networking group, get involved in that group and become known by the other members. Just joining a group really does nothing for your marketing. I volunteer at most events. That is the easiest way to become a familiar face to the rest of the organization and is much less expensive than a booth at trade shows or sponsoring some event. Other members get to know you on a very casual, personal level. When they do want to talk about financing, which is usually a pretty uptight stressful topic for most businesses, the barriers are already down. You've been there together folding the programs, setting up the tables, passing out the badges. You're not a stranger across the desk.

As the only alternate financing company at Women's Business Council (WBC), I am one of the standard panelists whenever there is a seminar on Access to Capital. Not only is this good exposure for me to the entire audience, but the rest of the panelists now have become good referral sources.

Website and Internet. The most important, most profitable, and most expensive marketing I do is internet marketing. I was very comfortable talking about money and factoring with people face to face, but knew zip about setting up a website. (I still don't.) We hired a professional we met through one of our Chamber memberships.

Dan very diplomatically showed what was wrong with the previous site we had done ourselves. Frankly, we did not know the first thing about working on the internet, and it showed. We had twirling gold dollar signs, jumbled text on every page, and other garish features that only loaded well on our computers, but not on the web. For a very modest amount (he was looking for new customers) he re-did our website and showed us all sorts of things to make web crawlers and search engines find our site. He did the search engine optimization, taught me how to set up pay per click campaigns, and how to budget my PPC money over an entire month.

When he started, Dan told us marketing successfully this way would take about six months, so we continued to go to some networking events. However, within six weeks, inquiries to our website had picked up (we had none before) and phone calls from our website continued to increase. We were filling the pipeline.

We analyzed the cost against the cost of the networking groups, and slowly dropped the network events and memberships. It was much nicer to sit at home, pick up the phone, write emails, and work in jeans. Plus we were covering the country now, not just the local area. This provided a much better chance for success.

As Dan improved the organic position of our website, the cost of the PPC went down drastically. Previously I was spending far too much per click. When I was either number one or two on the first page of each search engine, I got a lot of calls. They all asked a lot of questions and I gave out all the information I had. I probably closed 1-5% (which is nothing) of those prospects, and spent a good deal of money. With guidance from Dan I reduced my bids, taking them down to the minimum amounts. This can be $.03, $.05, or $.10 (that's the most I spend per click). My website is advertised most of the 24 hours period, because my daily budget is adequate with the lower PPC amount. My PPC expenses have gone down to $100-$300 per month, having been much higher.

If you decide to use your website as a marketing tool, rather than just an identification address, you need to research SEO (Search Engine Optimization) companies out there. There are hundreds – large, small, expensive, and cheap. Read about the companies and what they offer. Make a list of what is important to you. If you just want a home page you probably can do it yourself or get one of your children to do it for you. If you want to use it as a prospecting tool, you need to look at what you need, what you can or want to do yourself, and what your budget is. Call some of the companies and talk to them. Get written proposals, and also get references. Call and talk to the references. There are a lot of these companies who charge a lot, talk a lot, and deliver little.

When prospects find you on the internet this way, you must be prepared to answer questions, ask questions, and in a very short time establish a relationship and trust. Remember, these people are shopping. They have every funding source and every broker available to them with a click of the mouse.

So give them the floor. I always say literally, "The floor is yours. Tell me about your business, ask me about me. Whatever you want to do is fine." I stop there and start listening. You will probably hear a great deal that is totally useless to the final outcome. However, I have found that letting them tell me all about their business and what they are doing usually will influence them to stay with me. I am taking notes and I tell them. They like that; they are now important! Ask them questions – to whom are they are selling, etc., now that they are warmed up.

At a break or at the end of their recital, I ask if they have used factoring, have heard of it, etc. Depending on their response, I may give a brief overview and email them a couple of hand-outs I have used in seminars, or we may discuss their feelings of using factoring again. While I am on the phone I ask if they would like an application.

I always manage to ask about bank loans and IRS issues. If there is a long dead silence, I interject with, "It's fine, we work with the IRS." (By this time, I have a pretty good idea where I can place the prospect). If they are familiar with factoring, and I explain the option I can offer them, we go into whom they have talked to (since I don't want to duplicate efforts), where they factored before, and the reason for not going back there. Then I email them an application.

Regardless of the scenario, two days later I call them back. If I don't speak to them, I leave a message and also send an email. Just a gentle one, which says I am just checking back, do they have any questions, and are they still interested. Basically I keep going this way for about a month. If I don't have an application by that time, I stop the weekly email and they go into my next marketing program, direct mail, described below.

Direct Mail. No, my direct mail is not a list bought used to send letters. My list comes from the calls and emails from my website, and the contacts from WBC Networking. Yes, it has taken me a long time to build this list, but it keeps growing (though some on the list go out of business). Currently I have about 400 companies on the list.

I send everyone on the list a quarterly letter which just reminds them I am still around and still have financial resources who are actively funding businesses. It is one page, on my letterhead.

I personally sign (in blue ink) every letter. If I remember anything particular about the person, I also write a short personal note at the bottom. I keep notes in Outlook/Contacts, so it's not that hard.

The real reason this letter works is that it is sent in a green envelope, and I use transparent address labels. If your printer will handle this fairly stiff envelope, use the printer. Mine kept getting stuck, messing up envelopes, so I use the transparent labels, which take about ten minutes since the whole list is kept current in a mail merge document. My green envelope stands out from the white envelopes of other mail, and it looks almost individually addressed. I can tell from the results that it is opened.

The letterhead has all my contact information on it: name, company name, website, phone and fax numbers, email address, physical address. When you are establishing yourself from a phone call and/or a web site, the letterhead and contact information on the stationary give the prospect more confidence that you are real. I can count on getting at least five to ten calls or emails from this letter each quarter, and will usually close two or three deals from those calls. The letter also goes to people I have funded in the past and/or who are currently part of my funded clients. You do not drop them once you got them funded; you remember them. They have referred other clients to me. Once again, you have made them feel just a little special.

Yes, this does take quite a while to print, sign, and write notes; and I am constantly updating the list for the envelopes. I do around 25 or so every night while I'm watching TV or listening to my iPod. I try not to be doing this kind of work during the day, except for printing the actual letters. The workday is for the calls, emails and appointments. A sample letter is below.

As you can see, what makes this work is just the fact I am "touching them." About 4 weeks after a letter is mailed, I email people on the list, doing about 25 a day. It is personal, just asks them how they are doing, and to please contact me if I can help with any financing.

THE MONEY LADY
GUILIN GROUP, INC.

18718 Spring Grove
Dallas, TX 75240
www.guilinfunding.com

Phone: 972-934-1048
Toll Free: 1-877-872-4879
Fax: 972-960-6309
Email: agord@swbell.net

January (year)

IS YOUR BUSINESS CAUGHT IN THE CREDIT CRUNCH?
Your New Year's Resolution is to Grow Your Business.

The Government and Large Corporations are granting contracts and purchase orders worth hundreds of millions of dollars as we speak. You want to take advantage of these opportunities.

Are you able to get a piece of that business? Or are you waiting until you can save or borrow money?

Our funding sources are still solvent and are providing cash flow solutions every day.

We are ready to help you start your new year and grow your business. Don't let the bad news and the economic crisis slow you down.

You can have the best year you ever had!

To Your $ucce$$,

Anne Gordon

Anne Gordon, President
The Money Lady
Toll Free: 1-877-872-4879
Local: (972) 934-1048
www.guilinfunding.com

P.S. Call me - I am The Money Lady

Certified WBENC
Women's Business Enterprise

Cost depends on how many letters you mail; for me it is around $500 per quarter for postage, envelopes, paper, labels and ink. Colored envelopes are not inexpensive but they work. Also, the transparent/clear address labels are worth the extra money, versus the white label that everyone uses for every mass mailing. Do not use a really dark colored envelope. You have no choice but to put a white label on it, and it looks pretty tacky, especially after all your efforts to reach out and be personal. Aside from supplies the investment is the large amount of my time spent signing and writing notes. However, it has paid off so I consider it worth the effort.

What Somewhat Worked

Trade shows. For several years we bought a booth at every Buyer/Seller Trade Show within about 50 miles of where we lived. We had modest success, but once again it was tiring and expensive. We had a professional trade show display with spotlights. However, compared to the other financial companies exhibiting, ours was approachable. We had bright colors on it, and the banner above it said "The Money Lady."

That attracted a lot of people. However, for our own benefit (and it turned out to be a great way to keep the booth full) we had large multi-colored foam rubber floor tiles. I glued fake $1000 bills to the tiles. These tiles eased the pain of standing on a concrete floor for many, many hours. We also had a very large martini glass (about 12" high) filled with chocolate kisses of all colors.

People would want candy, and once they stepped onto the rubber flooring, they would look down see the money. They would begin to laugh, ask questions, and usually stay (mostly to rest their feet). However, the booth was always full, so anyone passing by would stop and come in to find out what was going on at our booth.

We also had Navy blazers with 'The Money Lady" embroidered in gold on the breast pocket. Everywhere we went we wore the blazers during the trade shows. Gene would also walk the aisles and visit/talk to every other exhibitor, collect cards and make notes to follow-up. The logo on the blazers always stopped people.

Now, we had all these names to follow up from each trade show. Yes, we prescreened them as we got their cards. The next two days were spent calling and emailing to follow up while the leads were still warm. Of course every other exhibitor was doing the same thing, so the attendees were being barraged with phone calls and emails. As long as we kept them on a list for later contact, we made some headway. However, for all the expense, time, and follow up effort, I believe that at least in our situation, the better route is the internet and direct mail to existing contacts.

Whatever your marketing plans are, they cannot be static. Our whole way of communicating and doing business is changing constantly. Always keep looking at new ideas and ways to promote your business. Then ask yourself, "Does it really work for you?" The comfort zone, especially in my case, must always be satisfied. Otherwise, it will not be worth the time, money, and effort you put into it.

What Didn't Work

Cold calling. I have tried cold calling from a list several times. I had a script and practiced, and it just did not work for me. I got very tired and frustrated trying to get to the right person and then engage them. I think because I was uncomfortable I had a high, squeaky voice and absolutely no conviction in my whole presentation. Now I will do anything other than cold call. I have to be comfortable with what I am doing and how I am doing it.

Post cards. My next marketing misadventure was caused by my lack of knowledge about the industry I targeted. Since I was living in Texas at the time with all the support companies who work for the large oil companies, I decided to target those companies outside the major cities who were between $2-5 million in sales.

The campaign consisted of two separate mailings. As I look back it was quite a lot of work for a prospect. I sent a large post card, which showed a website where they could submit their inquiry for financing. It linked to my website, and when they did clicked this link I would send a hand-written thank you note and a $5 Starbucks card. Shortly thereafter, the second mailing went out in letter form to the same people, with a few more words, but gave them a Due Date to submit an inquiry to the web site. I also had lists to follow up with phone numbers and names, which I did.

The campaign might have been very successful if I had checked to make sure my target group generated invoices! (They didn't.) I still shake my head when I look back at this. The problem: since most of the companies on my targeted list did not generate invoices, there was nothing to factor! So how were they paid?

The oil, gas, or natural gas pipeline system is on a meter. A delivery truck hooks up to the pipeline, the fuel is metered as it goes into the truck, and the meter stops when the connection stops. At a certain designated time, the commodity markets set the price, and 30-45 days later a check is mailed from the company picking up the fuel.

Did this campaign generate any response? A couple construction companies who were slightly interested, but nothing came of that. The cost of the printing was about $3,000 plus postage for two mailings of 1,000 recipients. This does not include my time calling all 1,000 names on the list. The return on investment was 0. It was an expensive lesson in doing my homework on a target industry to see if it can be factored *before* marketing to it.

Aside from the purchased oil field services mail list, I have not bought any lists. In today's internet world, if you really want to get a list with addresses, names and phone numbers, there are websites where you can get the lists at no cost. Yes, you have to copy/paste, or type them into some other program such as Word, but they are available. Without spending a dime, just go to www.manta.com, for example, type in janitorial companies, the city and state, and click Search. There is your list, and it gives you just about all you need.

Final Advice

Stay out there! So many times I have heard no one does any business in December and summer is a dead time. However, I have to ask: People don't work, bid on contracts and purchase orders during these times of the year? People don't need money in December for the holidays?

I have always kept my marketing going even during the economic downturns, the holidays, the summer time. Consistency works. It shows that I am still active, my business is still live, and my phone is still on. This is obviously a great time to reach out to existing prospects and clients, as well as start new relationships. Don't stop because everyone else does. This is your best time to shine.

RaeLynn Schkade

Integrity Factoring
www.integrityfactoring.com

Grandview, Idaho

RaeLynn Schkade grew up in Grand View, Idaho, and attended Boise State University where she studied finance. She and her husband Jens started Integrity Factoring in 2007. They work from their home in Grand View where they enjoy living in the country with their two young children. Family is central: they enjoy coaching little league soccer, basketball and baseball. They are involved in their community, church, and local 4-H program. RaeLynn enjoys volunteering in her daughter's classroom a couple of days a week.

Background

Before we started our factoring business, I was a stay at home mom and my husband was a truck driver. We were looking for a business that would allow me to remain at home with our daughter, have minimal startup costs, and eventually be profitable enough for Jens to quit his job and work in the business with me.

Our factoring business was not our first attempt at a home-based business. Just a year earlier we started a small freight brokerage business. This required me to find trucks to haul freight for manufacturers needing their products shipped. I did this from our spare bedroom that we turned into an office. I used the internet, a computer, a fax machine, and telephone. I did this for about a year; I didn't enjoy it and didn't make much money either. But while running this business I learned about factoring.

I would receive invoices from the truckers with a "Remit Payment to XYZ Factoring Company" stamp. I looked into what factoring was, how it worked, and what rates were charged. We came to the conclusion this would be an easier way to make money and we could use the same office space and equipment we already had. So I started offering a "quick pay" option to my clients as a way for us to practice factoring.

I liked this process much more than I did transportation brokering. We started our factoring business with a $5,000.00 loan from my grandma. In the meantime I bought Jeff Callender's books and studied factoring websites and factoring contracts to learn everything I could about how it worked.

It took me a year to get the factoring business started. It shouldn't have taken that long but I spent that year going back and forth, talking myself out of it one week, and then preparing to move forward the next. Two valuable lessons I learned from the freight brokerage business that served me during this process:

1. *Failure:* it is not that terrifying.
2. *Action:* all the preparing and planning in the world will not amount to anything if you don't act.

First, failure. My fear of failure in factoring was overcome when I realized failure was like a dark scary closet I was afraid to enter. But then a light flipped on and I found all that was there were some not so scary toys and clothes, and my fear disappeared. I also realized that beyond the fear of failure was something better – a business more suited to us.

Second, action. Action is the hard part, but it is the only thing that leads to results. I was feeling overwhelmed and having a hard time determining were to begin. I had to accept that I didn't have all the answers to everything; but I started small and learned one thing at a time. Each small success gave me momentum and motivation to continue to move in the direction of my goals. I would recommend starting where you are with what you have. The next step will always show up. It will be provided for you.

Marketing Strategy

Go with what you know. Our strategy from the beginning was to stick to what we knew. We both have a background in trucking. I grew up around it; my dad and brothers own and run trucks (although they had never heard of factoring). Jens worked with my dad for about five years driving truck.

Select a target market. We decided our target market as we started would be in the transportation business with volumes of $1,000 - $10,000 per month. This has since evolved from transportation to more specifically small trucking companies in oil field services. Our choice client is a hard working country boy with a few trucks. Our preferred volume now is $20,000 – $200,000 per month.

I would recommend choosing a factoring field in which you have some knowledge. It is much harder for someone to defraud you if you understand the work, the billing and all processes of that particular industry. If you understand that industry you will know the needs of people in it, and how to create a solution for them.

If you don't have a target market in mind before starting, I suggest factoring all kinds of different industries, and finding one you enjoy learning and in which you can become an expert. Plan on spending the time and effort to make yourself known in that industry's circles. Part of your marketing strategy could be to join an association or go to a trade show of your target clientele. I didn't do this but I did join an online Yahoo group and another web based group and contributed content.

Educate. I believe one of the best marketing strategies is not to compete with other factoring companies for the cheapest rates, but to inform and introduce your target market to the benefits of factoring. There is no shortage of small businesses needing working capital, but not everybody knows about this financing option.

We know the benefits of factoring first hand. In our fourth year of business we as a factoring company had to essentially "factor" the invoices we were purchasing due to our own lack of cash flow. In the factoring world this is called re-factoring.

For us it went like this. We found the clients and did the back office work (we were the "lead"), the other factoring company supplied the money and we split the income. By doing this we were able to grow six fold in one year. And those new clients will continue to bring us many new clients over the years.

We did not qualify for a bank loan: we had limited assets, not much experience, and had been in business less than five years. But we had a tremendous opportunity for growth and strong clients and debtors. The benefits we received from re-factoring this way are incalculable. There are many businesses in this same dilemma. Factoring is the solution for them.

Marketing Basics

Website. As you create a marketing plan, start with the basics. You must have a website with relevant information about your company and your services. Without a website, people have a hard time believing you exist. It is a place for potential clients to check out your legitimacy and see what you have to offer. So make sure your online presence is professional and helpful.

Business cards. You also need business cards. These are a must as you interact with colleagues and associates. You'll discover that just by talking and sharing your service with others, you will start to generate forward motion. Business cards make you readily available and easy to reach when someone realizes factoring is the answer to his needs.

Less Effective Methods

Direct Mail Letters. The first marketing I did, after the basics of a website and business cards, was to mail letters. I looked in the phone book under Transportation and mailed about 100 letters with my business card inside. It was a letter outlining all the benefits factoring would bring to their business. I was hoping to get a client without having to make any cold calls or appointments. I didn't get a single response. This took me about 8-10 hours and cost about $150.

Banner ads. We ran a flash banner ad on a trucking forum website for three months, but received only one phone call from the ad – and we never received the application back from that prospect. It cost us $800 and the time to come up with the ad. Its ineffectiveness could have been a combination of not the right place to put the ad, and not the right type of ad. We decided not to try this again.

Bankers. When we initially talked to our banker and explained what we did and the type of people we could help, we were hopeful we would receive leads from her. Logically this seemed like a great fit. She may have been the wrong loan officer to talk to, but I think this banker forgot about us and we received only one lead from her. If I was starting out again I would pursue this avenue further. I would visit different commercial loan officers from different banks. This doesn't cost anything but some business cards and time.

More Effective Methods

Larger factors. I had run (well there was nothing to run) the business for about four months and still didn't have any clients. I finally got so fed up with not having any clients that I worked up the nerve to call a large factoring company and asked them to send their "too small and too time consuming" leads. This was the first thing I did that was successful.

I Googled factoring and found a factoring company in transportation whose website mentioned monthly minimums (that means they require clients to factor a certain dollar amount each month.) I introduced myself and told the person I would be happy to look over their leads that didn't fit their criteria, and pay them 10% of the income I earned from these leads for the life of the account. I also told them that if the client outgrew me I would transition them back to the larger factor who gave me the lead.

I hit the jackpot and got many emails each week of potential clients to call. I only had $5,000 to begin with so I used that up quickly. One note on underwriting here: I was too cheap to get any credit checking or background reporting services at that time, so I was going on my gut feeling for underwriting. I would suggest using this method only if you love to lose money. The problem: the scammers are the exceptionally flattering and friendly ones. I still use my gut feeling but in combination with all the data I can get my hands on for a prospective account. A person's ability to judge others, when it comes to providing money, is perfected with experience, practice, and solid data in hand.

Our business grew very slowly at first, and as you have probably guessed, we lost money that first year which was tough. We had convinced a few other people to invest in our business. I remember one day lying on the floor in my office crying because I realized I had been scammed out of $16,000. I practically gave it to the crooked client. I was so eager to get my money on the street I did not do my due diligence or verifications properly. It could have been avoided with a little common sense, which I gained immediately!

I was calculating how many years of babysitting this was going to take to pay back my investors. Because I thought I didn't have what it takes to factor, I was giving up. But Jens believed in me and told me I was not going to pay this back with babysitting money. I was going to continue factoring. He told me this was a lesson that would make me stronger and better. It did indeed – and smarter and much more cautious! So I continued to factor, committed to analyzing things that weren't working, and to putting in place a different plan that would bring positive results.

Client referrals. As we started to get a few new clients we told them that for every company they referred to us whom we signed up, we would pay a referral fee of 10% of what we made from these accounts as long as we have them. I mailed our current clients our business cards so they could hand them out. Money tends to motivate people, and this brought us a few new clients.

Customer referrals. A similar strategy is to ask our client's customers to send us leads. Once we are comfortable with a customer's payment terms and history, we know there may be a steady stream of potential clients (their vendors) who need factoring. We send an email to the company's accounts payable person (the person getting harassed about when the checks will be sent), or to our contact at the company with whom we have become friendly. We provide our application to hand out as needed. This has been the second most successful marketing strategy we have used.

In the beginning all I had was time, so the very small and time-consuming clients for larger factors were perfect for our business. But as we have grown and tried to streamline our process, we are more interested in clients with predictable volumes and routine industry practices.

But I didn't want to just turn away the smaller guys. I knew these accounts would be profitable for the right person. I asked my sister, Andrea Owens, if she would like me to teach her to run a small factoring business from her home. She had loaned our business some money and was very content collecting her monthly interest. But she decided this could be a profitable little business for her. She started factoring and now makes a nice income.

The marketing strategy that works best for her is to build relationships with her good paying debtors. For some she offers a 10% referral fee, and for others she sends gift cards to their favorite restaurants a couple times a year. They are happy to refer her factoring service and love the ease that she has created for their accounts payable departments. They no longer have to deal with anxious clients wanting their money faster. Andrea handles that for them.

Provide exceptional service. The most successful marketing strategy we have is giving excellent, efficient service to our current clients. They in turn stay with us and tell their friends about us.

We don't have a program with just two options, take it or leave it. We are very flexible. When our clients come to us with special requests, we listen and then review their request. We can usually come up with some accommodation that satisfies us both.

We are available to answer their questions, we return phone calls that day, we are pleasant and upbeat, and we are knowledgeable about the industry. We don't put ourselves above them and/or profess to be financially sophisticated. We are empathetic to their needs, as we also are a growing small business. We share their same daily challenges and rewards. We look at our relationship with them as long term and we are open to how it can evolve for the benefit of both parties.

Our program does not require a term contract or monthly minimums. That is, we don't lock anybody in a contract for a certain amount of time, and they are not penalized for factoring less than a certain minimum volume each month. We make sure they don't feel like they are only there to benefit our profit margin.

I know when I am working with a business that is interested in my success and customizes solutions for me, I am loyal and happy to tell everybody I know how beneficial and great this company is. We do the same for our clients, and as a small business, this is our advantage over big businesses – our attention to detail and great service. We understand our clients' potential for our successes and use it fully. As a result, both parties win: we get loyal clients and our clients get exceptional service.

We know that people work with people they like. They will make a business decision by the way they feel and then justify it with their minds. If they can tell you understand their problem and have the solution, they will feel confident moving forward.

We know that success is not about having the lowest factoring rates. Someone who is solely shopping for the cheapest rates is not our target client. We don't have the cheapest rates. We are looking for people who need fair, prompt, convenient service so they can clear their minds of their cash flow problems and get to work on running their business.

This is same reason I outsource my accounting. I don't like the frustration nor do I have the skills or time to do it correctly. So I am willing to pay an "expert" to take care of that part of my business. Sure, I have to be involved but my accountant handles the hard stuff and makes it easy for me. That is the way we view cash flow for smaller trucking companies: we are their "experts." The client can be relieved of this frustration while we go to work on their behalf.

I have learned that as I stay focused on other people's needs, I make much more money than when I am focused on making money. In my first phone conversation with new potential clients, I ask a lot of questions. I know that when I call someone for their help, I like it when they are asking questions, taking notes and learning about my situation.

A typical first conversation includes questions like this:

- "What kind of business do you have?"
- "How long have you done this?"
- "How long have you worked with your customers?"
- "How long do they take to pay?"
- "Are there many customers or just one you want to factor?"
- "What are the amounts of your invoices?"

From this point I can usually tell if our program is going to work for them. If it is, I let them know this sounds like something we would be happy to look into further. If it's not, I tell them this really isn't our specialty but if they would like I could give them the name of another factoring company I think is better suited for their needs.

If they are a good fit I let them know how our process works. I tell them our discount and advance rates, ask them how they bill their customers, and explain we would customize a billing and verification process with them and their customers. I ask if they would like the application emailed or faxed and then I send a standard greeting with the application and a preliminary term sheet attached.

IFA meetings. A final marketing strategy that is fun and I thoroughly enjoy, and would recommend to anyone, is to attend International Factoring Association (IFA) meetings. I try to go to one a year. This is a great place to learn and network with like-minded people.

Summary

In summary, here are the marketing methods that have worked well for us.

1. Give great service to existing clients, and they in turn stay with us and tell their friends about us. We love that our business is based on helping others by providing a valuable service that can improve our clients' lives. We have worked very hard to build a solid reputation. Your name, your brand and your entire business can be quickly destroyed if you don't take good care of your clients and customers.
2. Build close relationships with account debtors and ask them to send any referrals they have that could benefit from factoring.
3. Call larger factoring companies and ask for their leads that don't meet their criteria. This costs us 10% of the discounts we earn for the life of an account, which is about 3% of our monthly net income.
4. Go to IFA conferences and network with other factors. This has provided us with great opportunities to associate with leaders and fellow entrepreneurs.

Advice

I encourage you to pick a couple of methods that seem to fit your business style and apply them now. This is an opportunity for you to clarify your purpose and create a vision and step forward toward making it happen. Ask yourself, "What am I trying to accomplish this year?" "What have I already done to try to improve my business, what has worked, and what has not worked?"

Be willing to try other methods, keeping in mind the discomfort caused by change is necessary for your growth. Keep your marketing plan simple and executable. Make a commitment to work hard and stay focused. Most people talk; few people act. Never forget that good results come slowly. Enjoy the process and results.

Our results: we now make more money in a month than we used to make in a year. My husband and I get to work in a business we thoroughly enjoy. I feel this has been a gift given to us and that I have an obligation to share what I have learned with others. I am passionate about factoring and am eager to help others succeed.

Marketing Methods for Small Factors & Brokers

Don D'Ambrosio

Oxygen Funding, Inc.
www.OxygenFunding.com

Lake Forest, California

Don D'Ambrosio grew up in Philadelphia and graduated from Temple University with a Bachelor's degree in Business Administration focusing in Accounting/Finance.

Prior to starting Oxygen Funding in 2007, Don was employed over 11 years with BNC Mortgage, Inc., a Lehman Brothers subsidiary, where he was Corporate Controller and Chief Financial Officer. He was responsible for all financial aspects of BNC Mortgage including budgeting, forecasting, proforma planning, financial statement preparation, cash flow analysis, taxes and external audits from CPA firms and regulatory agencies.

Oxygen Funding provides cash to qualified clients with short term cash flow needs through the purchasing of secured and reliable accounts receivable. The company looks at a client's profile rather than just an industry. Preferred clients have monthly volumes of $100k and below with room for growth.

The Need for Marketing

No matter what business you are in or which industry you cater to, without customers your chance of survival is basically nil. The cornerstone of any business consists of a solid marketing plan which focuses on attracting new customers in a cost effective manner to generate revenues and turn a profit.

Social Media

Way back in the day, (maybe six or seven years ago), most marketing plans consisted of an advertising budget, maybe some PR, a newsletter and occasional updates to the company's website. Depending on the size of the company, a marketing director could spend a small fortune on a basic "shotgun approach" where they place ads in local papers or trade magazines and hope that someone found it interesting enough to purchase their product or service. Just scan through the daily mail you receive at your home or office and you'll find flyers and postcards from companies trying to earn your business. I'm not saying these approaches are not effective, but with the advent of social media, many businesses with little or no budget can market their goods and services in a very effective manner.

Unless you live under a rock, almost everyone is familiar with social media and how it has changed the way we communicate with each other. Social networking sites such as Facebook have over 750 million subscribers with each user having an average of 130 friends. From a business perspective, entrepreneurs and developers from more than 190 countries build with *Facebook Platform*. As of this writing, Twitter has about 175 million subscribers that send over 456 "tweets" per second! There are many other forms of social media other than social networks such as podcasts, blogs, and RSS feeds to name a few.

What makes this social media movement so exciting for businesses is that any company looking to get noticed can do so with little or no money. Setting up an account with Facebook, Twitter or LinkedIn is free and a very good place to start. On LinkedIn, start by joining groups within your own industry to keep track of the latest news and events. Create a Facebook page for your business and get your friends and colleagues to "Like" your page. On Twitter, go to the "Who to follow" section and search for people and companies with similar interests.

Just as it is important to be part of social media for your business, it is even more important to participate by posting information with good content. What exactly does good content mean? Here are a few general guidelines that I like to use before I post information on our website:

1. Post useful information – this may sound like a no brainer, but you would be surprised how often I come across posts from friends and colleagues with no real point.
2. Entertain – try not to be boring. Liven up your post with some humor, or a personal experience on how you might have done something better.
3. Be an expert – know your facts about the topic so your followers look to you as a resource when they have questions.

What makes social media appealing to so many businesses is that there is no barrier to entry, little or no cost and you can use it as much as you want. Not a bad deal at all.

Press Releases

Another effective way to get your company noticed is to write a press release. According to Wikipedia, a press release is defined as "A written or recorded communication directed at members of the news media for the purpose of announcing something ostensibly newsworthy." The goal of the release is to generate interest in your topic and should be targeted to a specific audience and have a strong news angle. For example, if your company is in the invoice factoring business and you are launching a new service for a particular business segment such as government contractors, write about the benefits you will be providing and how it will help those within that specific industry.

For those of you who have never written a press release or may not be familiar with the format, I would start by reading a few actual releases online from some of the larger press release distribution companies such as *PR Newswire* or *Business Wire*. You can read a variety of press releases by subject, industry, company name, date, etc.

So how exactly do you write a press release? First, make sure the information in your release is newsworthy. Examples of newsworthy events can be the announcement of a new business startup, the launch of a new product or website, new events at your company or some philanthropic work your company has performed. Second, keep the reader's attention by focusing on how your company is providing a benefit to the targeted audience. Give specific examples of what benefits your company can provide readers. Share your success with readers and explain how you have achieved the growth and success you are writing about.

Do not craft your release to sound like a cheap advertisement for your company. Remember, you are trying to get your release picked up by media outlets and nothing turns off an audience more than fluffy self-promotion. It's also important to avoid technical jargon that will confuse and lose the attention of the average reader. A general rule of thumb is to keep the length to be somewhere around 500 words or less.

Now that you have written your release it's time for you share your information with the rest of the world. The easiest way to accomplish this is to utilize a distribution service which can do this at a reasonable cost. Just type "press release distribution services" into your favorite search engine and you will find ton of companies to willing to help you with this service. Most PR distribution service providers allow you to target specific media circuits based on geographic region and industry. The cost will vary depending on the length of your release and reach of the distribution. For example, the cost of a release to local media outlets will be less than one sent to a national circuit. Typically, a local press release of 500 words or less should cost less than $500 on average. Thus your budget will determine your exposure with this kind of marketing.

So ask yourself, "Is my company doing something newsworthy that others may find interesting?" For a relatively inexpensive cost, a well written press release can draw attention to your company and increase sales.

Marketing Methods for Small Factors & Brokers

Jeff Callender

Dash Point Financial Services, Inc.
www.DashPointFinancial.com

Tacoma, Washington

Jeff Callender grew up in Riverside, California, and graduated from Whittier College near Los Angeles with a Bachelor of Arts degree in Sociology. Jeff has been involved in factoring since January, 1994 when he began as a broker, working in that capacity for about seven months. He then ran his own small factoring business. Several years later he worked for a large national factoring company for about a year as an Account Executive. He started Dash Point Financial in 2001.

Dash Point Financial specializes in purchasing receivables of very small businesses; clients start near or under $10,000 in volume and grow from there. Dash Point funds transactions in various industries except for trucking, construction and third party medical receivables.

Jeff is also the President of FactorFox Software, LLC, which provides the cloud-based software platform, FactorFox. The data base is used by many factors of all sizes both in North America and around the world, and provides many additional services to its subscribers.

Definition of Marketing

Marketing is a word that describes the variety of means by which a company finds and brings in new clients to the business. Marketing can be intentional, random, and sometimes even accidental. The most effective methods of marketing are those which fit the type of business in which you work, attracts the interest of your preferred client base as efficiently yet cost effectively as possible, and suits a particular small factor's personality, skills, and interests. Marketing is a crucial element to any small factoring enterprise, for without it you have no clients, no income, and no business.

Best Marketing Methods

Over the course of my factoring career I've received the most number of referrals from four primary sources:

1. Brokers
2. Other factors
3. Website using good SEO
4. Writing books and articles.

Brokers. When I entered the factoring world as a broker in 1994, this was a natural way for me to obtain new clients as I started funding companies myself. I had a built-in network of broker colleagues I knew and with whom I had regular contact. Starting as a broker, I knew first-hand what a good broker needed to know and do when presenting referrals to factors, and learned to immediately recognize and value talented brokers when they sent me referrals. I also learned to train brokers in the type of deals I wanted and what they needed to do to make a good referral.

If a broker just dumps a prospect on my doorstep without bothering to prequalify or match them to my requirements, and isn't interested in simple instruction from me for the future, I don't want to work with that broker. Such people don't last long as brokers anyway. While this doesn't happen as much as it used to (there aren't as many factoring brokers as there once were – only the good ones survive), this does still happen occasionally.

I've streamlined my system for receiving broker referrals. My broker agreement is available on my website as a simple download. I require brokers to have a deal in hand before they complete and return it. Otherwise I'd have a boatload of completed broker agreements with no referrals from them, which is just a waste of the broker's time and mine.

I pay a 15% commission on all discounts I earn for the life of an account. Further, if a client referred by a broker in turn gives me a referral and I fund that new client, the original broker receives the 15% commission on the new client. I may or may not give the referring client a $100 finder's fee in this instance.

One reason I like getting referrals from brokers is I have zero marketing cost while the referral is still a prospect. That is, I don't pay anything out of pocket until a referral is factoring and I am earning income from the account. This just seems like a very cost-effective way to market, compared to throwing a lot of money into other methods just to find a prospect (most of whom don't close anyway). While paying brokers in the long run is a bit more expensive than other methods with upfront costs (especially if a client gets large and I'm paying 15% of a sizeable discount earned), I don't mind a bit – it means I'm making more. So the more I pay in broker commissions each month, the happier I am because it means I'm making more money.

I pay all broker commissions on the 10th of each month for the previous month's paid invoices. I don't pay commissions at the beginning of the month for two reasons.

1) I want to be sure the previous month's transactions have closed so I don't have any straggling commissions that might appear a few days after the first of the month. By the 10th, the recordkeeping is complete and accurate.

2) We pay investors and payroll on the first of each month and want to spread the workload so we're not overwhelmed paying people all at once. Also, delaying the broker commissions this way evens out my cash flow a bit in case I happen to be shorthanded on a particular month. This isn't much of an issue

any more but it was occasionally when my company was younger and smaller.

For the past many years I have been using FactorFox to track the sources of my leads, and throughout that time approximately 30% to 50% of my active clients have come from brokers. At the present moment the number is 31%, but that regularly changes over time.

Other factors. When I started back in the mid-90's, there were almost no small factors in business. I was practically the only one. This was a two-edged sword at the time; on the one hand, many larger factors didn't take me seriously and brushed me off as an aberration or a bit of a joke – I was not a real factor in their eyes. They didn't see how I could make enough money to run a viable business and considered me foolish because I was funding what they considered the dregs of the client pool: small, often high-maintenance, low-income accounts they certainly didn't want.

However, when I suggested I was very willing to take referrals from them when they found prospects who were too small – and would happily refer to them prospects too large for me – this got their attention. So did the idea that I would refer back the small deals I had incubated and grown to a level now acceptable to them. They realized I had something to offer and good referrals started coming.

I offered then, and still do, to pay my 15% commission on referrals from factors of any size. Larger factors often don't really want these commissions; they consider them too small, which can be the case. But some do accept.

I also provide such two-way referrals not only to larger factors, but to factors in particular niches that I don't fund. My business focuses on very small clients who want to factor around $10,000 or less to start, and many are mom and pop service businesses and young manufacturing and staffing companies. However I don't fund (no matter how small they may be) transportation, construction, and third-party medical receivables. I am happy to refer these deals to colleagues who specialize in these areas, and they in turn refer very small prospects to me that meet my criteria.

Also I receive referrals from (and give referrals to) other small factors who are in the same arena I am. While we are essentially competitors, this is good for both of us because it generates business for both. How?

- Sometimes my portfolio is full and I don't have the capital to accept a new client. If I refer a client to a colleague I'll receive a broker commission and still make some money on the deal.

- Sometimes I have a deal that has some aspect with which I'm not quite comfortable, but realize it could be a decent deal for someone else. Another factor may be hungrier for the business and willing to look at the prospect when I am not. Again, I receive a commission if it funds.

- The reverse of both these two instances is also true. There are some deals that colleagues can't or don't want to do, yet I may be quite interested. I welcome referrals like this. Of course, I always provide commissions for such referrals.

Approximately 20-25% of my active clients over the years have been referrals from other factors. I find this a great way to get new business. Presently 19% of my active clients were referred by other factors.

As others have mentioned, the International Factoring Association (IFA) provides great ways to increase your factoring knowledge and skills with its conferences and training workshops. These events are also fantastic networking opportunities to meet other factors with a wide variety of expertise, deal size, industry preferences, and referral sources of their own.

Likewise, some factoring software companies provide annual users meetings and conferences. Like IFA, these events provide not only excellent training in both factoring practices and how to get the most from your software, but terrific networking opportunities.

Website using good SEO. While I'm no computer expert and am not a programmer, some time ago I taught myself how to create websites and also good Search Engine Optimization methods. Being my own webmaster has saved me a great deal of money over the years since I don't have to pay someone to create or update my site. I have complete control over everything on my site and can update it any time I want for free. Besides, I really enjoy doing this.

Since my site has been up for many years and I implemented good SEO from the start, I have high organic rankings for my targeted search words with the major search engines. This brings a number of people to my site who call to inquire about my factoring services; some complete my application even before they call.

I am very careful on the first page of my website, and throughout it is well, to clearly define my factoring niche, state plainly the types of factoring deals I fund, as well as those I *don't* fund. This enables the people who arrive at my site to weed themselves out if they're not a good fit before I ever talk to them. Thus I don't get too many inquiries from people who are a mismatch; they've already pre-screened themselves. I do get a few "shoppers" but for the most part, people who call recognize that I will fund their very small companies, unlike most larger factors with whom they've already spoken.

My application form is on my site and if people are interested in factoring with Dash Point Financial, I don't have to send them anything. They just fill out the form and I receive it in seconds via email. Their data is already pre-entered into FactorFox's CRM system and I don't have to copy and paste their information into my software. I can simply talk to them and begin my underwriting as soon as I've received their data, and determined they are a likely fit.

When I do get a "shopper" this usually becomes apparent early in the conversation ("How much do you charge?" is usually the first or second question they ask). If I get the sense that all they are interested in is the lowest rate, I tell them quickly they can probably find cheaper rates elsewhere if that's all they really want. But I also tell them that many factoring rates advertised on the internet don't include hidden fees and additional charges, and often include an application fee, long term contracts and monthly minimums – all of which are absolutely true. Dash Point has no application fee, hidden fees, long term contracts, or monthly minimums. This usually makes my total charges competitive or even less than another company with "lower" rates.

I give them a list of questions to ask the other factors they're considering, and see who offers the best overall program for what they need. I don't try to sell them on Dash Point, though I do point out our advantages; I just do all I can to help them make the most informed decision they can. Thus I'm acting more like a consultant, helping them figure out which factor or other means of financing is best suited to their situation.

I'm truly trying to help them, not just convince them to factor with me. This comes across and people sincerely appreciate my effort. If Dash Point turns out to be the best match, they are all the more ready to work with me. If they mention the name of another factor they're considering and I know the company is solid, I tell them so: "That's a good company. If you decide to go with them you'll be in good hands."

Thus I spend time educating "shopping" prospects as to what factoring companies really need to earn to mitigate their risk and be profitable, and at the end of the day, the total amount they're paying usually won't be that much different from one factor to another. What they really need to be looking for is a factor who will provide excellent service, promptly respond to their needs, be trustworthy, have rates and procedures that are reasonable and simple to understand, and have staff people with whom the prospect will want to work for the next several months if not years.

Believe me, this whole approach goes a long way. It's not selling, it's educating. And educating is a far more effective marketing method for a small factoring company than pressing a prospect in order to "close the sale."

When I first started developing my website it took some time to learn how to make it look professional and utilize good SEO methods; this has paid off quite well over the years. Now my website costs in both time and money are extremely low and I receive a good number of solid referrals from it. Approximately 20-40% of my active clients over the years have been direct self-referrals from my website. Presently 38% of my active clients found me through my website. These leads are virtually free now since there is no broker commission and no webmaster to pay.

Writing books and articles. When I first became a factor, there were literally no books written on the subject for the general public. In the very early days of the internet in the 1990's, I found a little publication printed on typing paper, obviously hand-assembled, and resembling a term paper I would have turned in back in my college days. It was quite simple yet well written by someone who was a small factor. I paid $50 for it and immediately realized I could write something more thorough. I could write a real book that would cost less and have much better reach. I realized if I gladly paid $50 for this, I could provide a better resource for less money and it would sell. I learned how to self-publish (just like I learned how to create my website and do proper SEO) and set out to become a self-published author.

I wrote my first book, *Factoring Small Receivables*, and published the first edition in 1995, selling the book privately and later through a fledgling online book seller named Amazon. I continued to update the book every couple years and each new edition included new and revised information. Each new version also looked more professional (evolving progressively from a 3-ring binder, to wire-bound, to paperback, to a PDF ebook, to tablet ebook formats). After seven editions, I changed the name of the book's 8th edition to *How to Run a Small Factoring Business* to make it more descriptive of the content.

Meanwhile, in the course of earlier editions of the first book, I realized that a book series was really needed to more completely educate people about factoring, how it helps businesses, and how people can become small factors themselves. (Many of the contributors to this book became factors after reading these books.) Over the course of a few years I wrote several more titles which are listed on "Also by Jeff Callender" page at the beginning of this book.

My purpose for writing was not to make money from writing and selling books. Unless you're a big-name author with a major publisher, that doesn't happen. Rather, my reason for writing was simple: I wanted people to know about factoring. I have always found it a fascinating business, a wonderful tool for starting and growing clients' companies, and a sorely needed service by a huge number of small firms. I didn't stop to think that becoming an author would actually become an excellent means of marketing.

By this time Amazon.com was becoming a household name, and when I saw that there were literally no books on factoring being sold there, I realized I was sitting on a remarkable opportunity. I set about writing books on every angle of factoring I could think of. I didn't bother going to an outside publisher because I had learned enough about the publishing world to know that would be an exercise in frustration. So I learned how to self-publish and sell my books on the internet through Amazon and my own publishing company's website, DashPointPublishing.com.

This worked well and my books, as well as articles I often wrote for various factoring and cash flow-related publications, resulted in something I quite honestly didn't anticipate: I had become an authority on the subject. I was the *national expert* on factoring small receivables. This opened many doors and gave me excellent name recognition and branding for both my books and my factoring business.

It also gave, and continues to give, instant credibility when I speak to prospective clients who ask about my experience and knowledge of factoring. Prospects who ask this question are posing a more direct demand: "Do you know what you're doing? Do you really know how to handle my account, or are you going to make mistakes that can hurt my business?"

When I'm asked this question I say I've been in factoring since 1994 and mention I've written several books on factoring that are sold on Amazon, which have been used by many, many people to start their own factoring companies. No one else can say this and the client realizes I am as experienced as anyone they'll find, and certainly know what I'm doing. That is a tremendous competitive advantage and a unique and powerful way to market my business.

While I can't give any kind of statistics or numbers of clients and referrals I've received from writing books and articles over the years, doing so has been the foundation of my life as a factor and my core marketing method from the beginning – though it was admittedly by accident when I started. It has made me what I am in the factoring world today, and will continue to provide referrals and many other opportunities for as long as I'm in the business.

Somewhat Effective Methods

Leads group. When I first started factoring I joined a networking group called LeTip. This group is very similar to BNI: it is a structured national organization, its local chapters meet weekly for breakfast or lunch, only one type of business is allowed in each chapter, and its whole purpose is to pass leads between members.

I was part of the group for a couple years and received some leads, but nothing to set the world on fire. The reasons for this were:

1. Most of the people in my group were involved in real estate, and they just didn't have much contact with small business owners who would be prospective clients for me. They were involved with selling houses, providing mortgages, and so on; not working with small businesses.

2. At that time (mid-1990's) almost nobody in the group had heard of factoring, and most of the members never really quite grasped what I did, despite my weekly 30-second commercials and occasional 10-minute presentations. I received an occasional lead from the attorney, but the poor quality of the leads showed he really didn't "get" factoring.

3. The couple members who should have given me leads – the accountant and banker – did not. The accountant was arrogant and acted like he knew everything about finance, and never said a word (positive or negative) about factoring to the group. Neither he nor the banker were factor-friendly. They simply never referred anyone to me.

The quarterly regional meetings were somewhat better. Several chapters from the region met at once and everyone gave a 30-second commercial to the whole group of about 100 people, instead of just 15 or so at the weekly chapter meetings. I gained a few leads from these; but overall, for the amount of time, energy, and expense I put into the group, I eventually concluded my particular group wasn't worth it and dropped out. By that time my broker and factor networks were working well, and I didn't feel the need to put the effort into finding a better leads group that would be more beneficial.

However, I did appreciate the potential value of such groups. If I had been in a vibrant chapter with a factor-friendly accountant, banker, insurance agent, attorney, and service companies who had colleagues in need of my service, this would have been highly valuable. The trick is finding a good group with the right mix of people.

However, don't assume a group's banker, accountant, lawyer, and other such members will give you leads. Before you join a group, speak to these particular members privately and learn what they really think about factoring. If they view it negatively (as some will), keep looking. You'll be wasting your time in a group with people who should be your primary source of referrals, but have an unfavorable attitude about what you do.

Clients. I regularly tell clients, especially when they are just starting with me, that I gladly give finder's fees for referrals they've given me that become my clients. Usually this is $100 per referral after I have made that much in discounts from the account. Sometimes these referrals are poorly pre-qualified, but other times they can be quite good leads.

If a client is in a position to give excellent, well qualified leads (like a good broker), I may offer to pay an amount similar to what I pay professional brokers, especially if they are highly money-motivated. However, I want my clients to focus primarily on running their business smoothly so we both make good, dependable income together. I don't want them getting sidetracked and spending an inordinate amount of time finding leads for me. I want their companies to be factoring successfully, first and foremost.

Customers. While I don't make a point of contacting clients' customers and asking for referrals (this probably works better for trucking factors as RaeLynn found), occasionally I do get such referrals. These usually come from companies whose vendors (my prospects) are somewhat financially unstable, and they need these people to dependably do their work but can't pay them promptly. When they see how factoring stabilizes these companies and that Dash Point is great to work with, we get occasional referrals from them.

This isn't a bad way to get referrals, as long as you are confident in the stability of the debtor. You also must be careful not to develop an over-concentration of funds with a particular debtor with numerous clients whose invoices you're factoring.

Public speaking. Over the years I have led a number of workshops and training sessions that deal with factoring. Most of these audiences have been other factors and brokers, which again has helped establish my role as an authority about factoring. While I haven't spoken to local business groups, this is certainly a good means of educating potential leads and referral sources about factoring, and marketing your business locally.

Banner ads. I haven't done too many of these and have avoided Pay Per Click with Google Ads and other quite expensive providers. This is because I haven't felt the need to pay for Google Ads when I'm already ranked #1 or #2 organically for my key search words on that search engine anyway. However, occasionally I'll place a banner ad on a very carefully selected website whose primary audience is brokers and other smaller factors.

Telemarketing. Cold calling leaves me cold. I would rather have a root canal than spend an hour making cold calls. Obviously, this is not in my comfort zone.

However, I have no problems at all with someone else making such calls *for* me. I experimented with a telemarketing service making calls on my behalf to set appointments for my staff to speak with the prospect. When I received the list of people interested in speaking with my company, one of my staff made a follow up call and determined if the person was both serious and a bona fide prospect.

The telemarketing company I used employed a caller who unfortunately was ineffective. This was a person who didn't really understand factoring, and I'm sure she'd never owned a business.

Thus the idea of selling invoices was foreign to her, and it took her too long to catch on to how to cold call my prospects. I terminated the service as it wasn't inexpensive, the results were poor, and I was receiving qualified leads through other channels anyway.

However, I saw from this experience how a really good telemarketer could produce very strong results. When I'm in the position of needing new business in the future, I'll look for a telemarketer through Elance.com or another similar service. There are plenty of qualified telemarketers listed there.

Below is a graph and table of where my currently active clients originated.

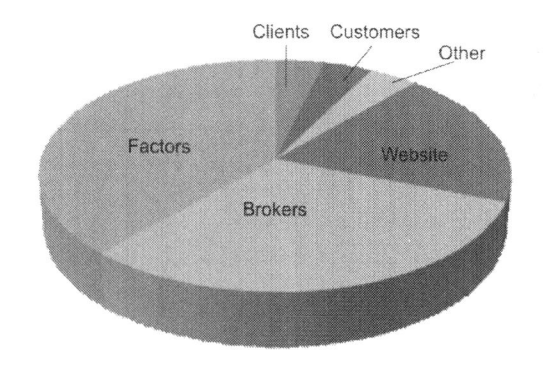

Clients	4%
Customers	4%
Other	4%
Factors	19%
Brokers	31%
Website	38%
	100%

Methods That Have Not Worked

Leads websites. I have tried a handful of leads generating websites with little success. These are sites that promote factoring as a means of financing businesses, and prospects register for free and complete a form that describes their business and financial needs. The leads are then sent to factors who match the criteria the prospect is seeking by industry, volume, location, and so on.

In the most recent one, I paid $1,000 for about 30 leads which were people looking to factor their receivables with a volume of less than $10,000. The majority of these referrals never answered our phone calls and did not respond when my staff left both a phone and email message. Some of those we reached were unqualified as factoring prospects (they provided swimming lessons, volleyball training, piano lessons, were just "thinking" about starting a business, had no business or government invoices, or just weren't quality business owners). I closed one client from this campaign who has a rather difficult debtor.

Radio ads and radio guest spots. Several years ago I decided to host an educational seminar about factoring and promoted it via radio ads. It was kind of cool hearing my ad and company name over the radio, and the phone rang immediately after the ads aired with people wanting to register. Some didn't show up at the seminar (no surprise) and we ended up with about five or six people sitting around the table. However, none of them became clients and I felt the effort was unproductive.

I've also been interviewed on a very small local internet radio business show, as well as with a larger business radio show in the Northeast who was doing a piece on factoring. The host did a live interview with a client of mine who lived there, and me. I didn't feel I spoke very well (since it was live there were no "re-do's"), and it generated just one request for a free book which I gave as incentive to call me, but no client referrals. While it was an ego boost, it generated no new business.

Marketing Costs in Dollars and Time

The cost of broker and factor commissions each month vary with the income their referrals generate, of course. We pay between $1,000 to $5,000 for monthly commissions to brokers and other factors. Over the course of the year this adds up to between 8% to 11% of annual revenue. Again, this is a noteworthy expense but is only owed when income has been earned, it is not a fixed expense, and it accounts for about half of the active clients we have.

We spend very little or nothing for other marketing methods, which account for the other half of the clients in our portfolio. Since the other source that brings in the most referrals – our website – costs practically nothing, I like getting referrals from that source.

The three main sources of our clients – referrals from our website, brokers, and factors – take very little time. The only time these require is spent actually talking to prospects; I spend virtually no time or money just getting to that first conversation. Since I'm not spending long hours at group meetings, mixers, and the like, almost of my time is spent in the office tending to business, determining which clients I'll accept, and underwriting them. This is the kind of marketing I prefer and it has worked well over the years.

Elevator Speech

I have a few elevator speeches, depending on the audience. Below are four of them that can be used with nearly anyone.

- "My company provides financing for very small business owners who are turned away by banks. Instead of providing loans, we purchase our clients' invoices for immediate cash which enables them to meet payroll, pay bills, accept larger customers, and many other business necessities."

- "My business supplies something every company needs: money! Our clients have invoices that take 30 days to pay, and we purchase their invoices with cash advances within 24 hours of the invoices being created. We've helped hundreds of businesses get started, grow quickly, and operate profitably."

- "I finance very small companies by buying their receivables at a small discount, as soon as their invoices are created. This enables my clients to increase their cash flow quickly, without generating debt. Our clients are small business owners who have been turned down for bank loans."

- "My name is Jeff Callender, my company is Dash Point Financial Services, and I get paid to wait! I work with very small business owners who wait 30 days to receive payment from their business or government customers. I buy the rights to their payments, give them an up-front advance, and then wait for their customers to pay me. This enables my clients to give 30 day terms yet still get paid tomorrow.

Advice

Unless you come from a marketing background, this part of your factoring business can be one of the most difficult, and you face it immediately when you start your operation. Unless you have a built-in pipeline of prospects (which some people do from a previous business or career), figuring out which marketing methods fit your style and personality – and actually work – is usually not easy and can often take a fair amount of time.

When you start, begin with what you are good at and *like* to do. Don't try to use a method that you inherently dislike, or at which you are decidedly untalented, whatever that may be – cold calls, public speaking, writing, whatever. I'm sure you can name it out loud right now. But if particular methods come naturally for you, chances are good you can use them effectively and marketing can actually be enjoyable and produce positive results.

Part 3

Analysis

Analysis

Assessment

Thus far our contributors have described marketing methods that have worked for them, other methods that haven't worked as well or at all, described their marketing costs, given advice for newcomers, and mentioned some resources they have found helpful. In this chapter, we will pull all this information together so their methods can be cataloged and analyzed.

Below are two summary charts compiled from all writers' contributions. Specific resources found helpful and mentioned by each are condensed into the first chart, the Resources Chart. It is sorted alphabetically and lists resources described by the writers. It includes the type of resource described, where it can be found, and which writer/s mention/s the resource.

Marketing Methods for Small Factors & Brokers

Resources Chart

Resource	Type	Where	Mentioned By
American Club Assoc.	Business group	www.acanetwork.org	Kim
Business Network International (BNI)	Networking group	www.bni.com	Melissa
Business Wire	Press release distribution	www.businesswire.com	Don
Constant Contact	Email blasts	www.constantcontact.com	Kim
Elance	Job matching site	www.elance.com	Jeff
Facebook Platform	Facebook page development	www.facebook.com/platform	Don
FactorFox	Factoring software	www.FactorFox.com	Jeff
International Factoring Association (IFA)	Professional association	www.factoring.org	Kim, Melissa, Tony, RaeLynn, Jeff
LeTip	Networking group	www.LeTip.com	Jeff
Manta	Company lists	www.manta.com	Anne
National Assoc. of Women Business Owners (NAWBO)	Business group	www.nawbo.org	Kim
PR Newswire	Press release distribution	www.prnewswire.com	Don
Reference USA	Business lists	www.referenceusa.com	Kim
Referral Institute, The	Referral training	www.referralinstitute.com	Melissa
Small Factor Series, The	Books	www.DashPointPublishing.com	RaeLynn, Anne, Jeff
Toastmasters	Public speaking	www.toastmasters.org	Kim
Women's Business Council	National certification	www.wbenc.org/	Anne

Next a digest of all the marketing methods described in this book is found in the Marketing Methods Chart. This chart summarizes the methods mentioned and indicates writers' experiences as to each method's effectiveness, cost, and time required.

With this chart we can glean which tools have proven to be most and least effective for the contributors, remembering most methods received mixed reviews. The reader can use this chart to help determine which methods may be best suited to his or her marketing efforts.

The methods are listed alphabetically. Next to each method is the number of contributors who mention using the tool, and their evaluation of its effectiveness, cost, and time required. For example, in the category "Direct Mail" one person found the effectiveness of this method to be high, and two found the effectiveness to be low. One felt the cost was moderate and two found the cost high. All three said the time required for this method was high.

To assist, the chart is color-coded. The green (left) columns in each section indicate the most desirable ranking. The yellow (middle) columns indicate moderate ranking, and the orange (right) columns indicate the least desirable ranking. Thus, look for methods that have the most numbers in the green (left) columns, and the fewest numbers in the orange (right) columns. Those with the most effectiveness, least cost, and least time are the most valuable.

While the number of people involved in this comparison is too small to be statistically significant, you do see where the contributors stand, and can gain insight from their experience and opinions.

Marketing Methods for Small Factors & Brokers

Marketing Methods Chart

Marketing Methods	Effectiveness			Cost			Time			Mentioned By
	High	Moderate	Low	Low	Moderate	High	Low	Moderate	High	
Ads:										
Magazines/Bus. Journals			3			3	3			Kim, Melissa, Tony
Radio			1		1		1			Jeff
Become the Expert	3			3			3			Kim, RaeLynn, Jeff
Cold Calling			2	2					2	Kim, Anne
Direct Mail	1		2		1	2			3	Kim, Anne, RaeLynn
Educate	1			1			1			RaeLynn
Exceptional Service for Clients	2			2			2			Ryan, RaeLynn
Good Will	1			1			1			Melissa
Groups										
Business Groups		1		1			1			Kim
Networking Groups										
Chamber of Commerce	1	1	1		3			1	2	Kim, Tony, Anne
Leads Groups	2	1	1		4				4	Kim, Melissa, Tony, Jeff
Women's Business Council		1		1			1			Anne
International Factoring Association	3			3			3			Tony, RaeLynn, Jeff
Internet										
Banner Ads			1			1	1			RaeLynn
Blogs		1		1			1			Kim
Email (to stay in touch)		1		1				1		Kim
Facebook Ads	1				1		1			Ryan
Facebook Page	2	1		3				2	1	Melissa, Ryan, Don
Leads Websites			1	1			1			Jeff
LinkedIn Page		1	1	2				2		Kim, Melissa
Pay Per Click		1	1			2		2		Kim, Anne
RSS Feeds	1					1	1			Kim
Twitter	2			2				2		Ryan, Don
Website	2		2	3		1	4			Melissa, Tony, Anne, Jeff
Lunch & Learn meetings	1			1			1			Kim
Post Cards			1			1			1	Anne
Press Releases	1			1			1			Don

Marketing Methods	Effectiveness			Cost			Time			Mentioned By
	High	Moderate	Low	Low	Moderate	High	Low	Moderate	High	
Public Speaking	2			2				1		Melissa, Jeff
Referrals:										
Accountants, CPAs	1		1	1		1		1	1	Ryan, Tony
Bankers	1		2	3			3	1		Ryan, Tony, RaeLynn
Brokers	3				3			2	1	Kim, Tony, Jeff
Clients	1	1			2			2		Tony, RaeLynn
Clients' Customers	1			1			1			RaeLynn
Other Factors	4			4			4			Melissa, Tony, RaeLynn, Jeff
Turnaround Consultants	1			1				1		Ryan
Sales People (in-house)		1				1		1		Melissa
Seminars to Business Groups	2			1	1					Kim, Melissa
Telemarketing			1			1	1			Jeff
Trade Shows		1				1		1		Anne
Write Articles, Books	2			2				1	1	Kim, Jeff

Marketing Methods Analysis

As we analyze the information, one point stands out: there is no silver bullet for marketing a small factoring business. In other words, no single method works 100% of the time for everyone. Some use a particular marketing strategy very successfully, while others have found the same method unrewarding.

Thus, before you resort to the Spaghetti Technique without any forethought, first carefully analyze your particular skills and make a reasoned decision as to which few marketing methods will likely be most effective for *you*. As Kim suggested, start with no more than three, and give each method at least six months of serious effort before you decide it doesn't work. Then make the same reasoned, logical decision when selecting something else. Again, give it time to prove or disprove itself.

For our contributors, what has worked the most and least effectively? Let's take a closer look.

High Effectiveness. The most often mentioned method with high effectiveness (4), interestingly, is somewhat counterintuitive: other factors. While some people may want to have little contact with companies they consider competition, at least four writers don't think this way. They have found the best source of referrals to be colleagues who are both in other niches, as well those vying for the same prospects. They have found that most people in this industry are much more collegial with – instead of wary of – each other. What's more, referrals from other factors also cost the least (4) and take the least time (4), making this method the overall most desirable among our writers.

In part this explains why the next most effective method (listed by 3 as highly productive) is the International Factoring Association (IFA). While activity there doesn't put you in direct contact with prospective clients, its networking opportunities introduce you to other factors. When you combine that with the excellent training workshops and conferences IFA provides, being active in the organization makes complete sense. However, simply joining IFA and never attending any events is of much less value. You need to come to events and take advantage of the opportunities in person to get your money's worth.

Another method also mentioned by three writers as highly effective is Become the Expert. Kim, RaeLynn, and I all found this an excellent way to position yourself, especially in your local community or among your client base, as a way to bring in new business. If people are confident in your expertise and professional skills as a factor of your particular niche or specialty, you brand your name, and clients are likely to be very comfortable choosing you. Further, you will get more referrals from brokers and other factors who recognize you as the expert in your specialty.

The other most effective marketing methods among our writers is receiving referrals from brokers. While a couple writers intentionally steer clear of brokers, three find them one of the most effective means of getting referrals. The difference in opinion here is probably due to good or bad broker experiences each writer has had. While those who have dealt with top quality brokers appreciate their leads (and the fact there is no out of pocket cost up front), those who have dealt with brokers who do a poor job learn to avoid their leads. They don't want to waste time on unqualified leads an unsatisfactory broker may present.

The next marketing methods, with two people considering each highly effective, are Leads Groups, your company's Facebook page, Twitter, Website, Public Speaking, giving Seminars to Business Groups, and Writing articles and books.

The Leads Groups method received among the most mixed reviews, with four people having used them, and two ranking them highly effective, one moderately effective, and one with low effectiveness. Like many of the methods that writers considered most effective, those who became deeply involved in a method (notably Melissa is a regional leader in BNI) found them most effective. Because such groups take a considerable amount of time (4 with High in the Time column) and a fair amount of cost (4 with Moderate in the Cost column), making these groups work clearly take a serious commitment.

With any group, getting deeply involved usually results in viewing the time spent as more worthwhile. Kim, Melissa, and Anne all make a point of doing a lot more than just showing up at the regular meetings. Melissa spends time at BNI's regional level promoting the group (and thereby her business), and Anne has made a point of volunteering for set up and break down of meetings, thereby coming to know other members on a more basic level than just sitting around a table.

As Kim puts it, "The best way to make your...experience beneficial is to get involved. The other...members need to see you active and involved. This will help you begin to build relationship with the various members who are your new referral sources. Join a committee, or volunteer for a leadership position ...to get the most out of your membership."

The two who find Facebook and Twitter to be highly effective (Ryan and Don) are quite skilled and know how to make the most of this technology. Others who mentioned these methods said they don't know enough about them to be useful, which is actually true for most any marketing method. The more you know about how to use a particular marketing tool, the more you appreciate how it works and how to use it to your greatest advantage. The other big benefit of Facebook and Twitter (once you know how to use them) is they are free. The only real expense is your time, unless you hire someone to manage these for you.

Likewise, with Public Speaking, Giving Seminars to Business Groups, and Writing, the two writers who found these highly effective were already skilled in these areas. Public speaking is one of the most feared activities by most people in the general public; if you're already good at this, you should make the most of it. If public speaking is sheer agony, don't torture yourself and try to make it work for you just because it works for someone else. You'll experience the equivalent of Anne's "squeaky voice" when she made cold calls: it will be absolute misery for you and very ineffective.

The same is true with writing: some people are natural writers and cranking out pages of copy is second nature. Others must sit at the keyboard for hours just to get a couple sentences out. Their difficulty with expression, grammar, spelling, and punctuation would make any editor cringe. Again, as RaeLynn put it, "Go with what you know." Don't use a particular method only because someone else is good at it. Do what *you* do well.

Low Effectiveness. The least effective method mentioned by three writers (the most of any method), was placing **Ads in Magazines/ Business Journals**. What's more, these ads are acknowledged as High in the Cost column by all three writers. While print ads are sometimes favored by brand new small factors, this method's ineffectiveness and high cost make it something to skip.

On the other hand, a few factors (none who wrote for this book) who have used print ads successfully are very particular with this method. They've placed small, less expensive ads for a long, consistent run in small local business journals. They don't place them in large newspapers or magazines, and especially don't run them just once. The small publications charge less and have a much more targeted audience: business owners near the factor. As Melissa mentioned, they may allow you to write an article for the publication. The key is running the ads consistently over a long period of time to a narrow, identified audience.

Several other methods were mentioned by two writers with low effectiveness. These include Cold Calling, Direct Mail, Website, and

Referrals from Bankers. Interestingly, the latter three were also found to be High in Effectiveness by one other writer. Thus, we have very mixed reviews for what *doesn't* work, as well as for what does. Interesting!

How did one person find these three methods highly effective, while two found each very ineffective? Let's look at these three.

Kim and RaeLynn found **Direct Mail** very ineffective. Kim purchased a canned list that wasn't cheap and had several outdated entries. RaeLynn pulled 100 names out of the phone book listed under Transportation, her factoring niche. It took her many hours to prepare the list, create and stuff the letters, and cost $150. Both sent their letters to strangers – people with whom they had no previous contact, and both received virtually no response.

However, Anne – who uses direct mail quite successfully – uses a mailing list she has developed herself over the years, made up of people with whom she has had direct contact. Further, she "dresses up" her mailings – sent quarterly to her whole list of about 400 – in green envelopes that stand out from regular mail that arrives in white envelopes. She uses the same letterhead each time which makes each piece familiar to her recipients, who receive about four of these a year. While the look is familiar, each letter has a seasonal slant to her message: she's The Money Lady, ready to help them whenever they need funding. Great branding!

What's more, Anne sends the letters to people she's already helped fund, not just prospects. Clients remain on her list so she can keep in contact with them on a regular basis. This keeps her before them not only when they need money, but when a friend or colleague of theirs does. As a broker, this is a very astute way to do that. Moreover, Anne not only hand-writes her signature in blue ink on each letter, she even adds a personal note. Thus her letters are not "junk mail" in the eyes of her recipients, but a real letter with a short handwritten message from a finance professional. With ordinary junk mail and the massive amount of email spam we all get these days, this must be refreshing to the people on her mailing list, each of whom know her.

Anne's letters are a lot of work and go miles beyond the standard direct mail piece, but for her the time and effort pay off. And since she can do these mailings in the evenings while watching TV or listening to music, she doesn't mind. Would this work for people with little kids and/or a spouse not involved in the business? Probably not, but it works for Anne. That's the key.

While Melissa and Tony rightly believe their **Website** is needed to be considered legitimate in the factoring world, both find it an ineffective means of marketing their service. Melissa doesn't want clients to find her website directly because she wants to deal with prospects in her geographical region and who come from a trusted, face-to-face referral source (in her case, BNI). Tony considers his site to be a brochure which thoroughly describes his company to people who are considering his service, but not really a means of bringing in clients in the first place. Thus neither spends much time on their site as they have other methods of finding prospects which works better for them.

The reason I find my website to be highly effective bringing in new prospects is because, like Anne, I have spent quite a bit of time and effort to use this method for the greatest benefit. While Anne (happily) pays her webmaster to manage her site and SEO, I chose to learn to do this myself. Both ways can work, as long as your webmaster/you are good at it, not overpriced, and produce positive results.

When I started my marketing efforts, I enjoyed working on website design (it fit my personal interests) and learned everything I could about how to do it properly. I read about search engine optimization techniques and how to use them in websites. Over the years, I have continued with these and maintain my websites to keep my high organic rankings. It's not something Anne and I did once and stopped; it has been a continual marketing process over the years that, for us, has worked.

While Ryan does not go into great detail as to how he makes **Referrals from Bankers** and CPAs highly effective, he states one crucial sentence: "The key is creating a lasting working relationship." Doing this takes time, persistence, and constantly keeping your face and name before your audience. This is what Ryan does with bankers, what Anne does with her letters, what Melissa does with her BNI associates, and what every writer does who has found a particular marketing method that works especially well.

Each has found, and constantly uses, one or more methods that keep them in front of leads (or sources of leads) to create "a lasting working relationship." That is the key to successfully marketing a small factoring business or factoring broker business. The lesson here – and message of this book – is that successful marketing does not result from what method you use; it results from *using a method that fits your personality and skills, and doing it all the time* to form and keep lasting working relationships.

Conclusion

Conclusion

We discovered early in this book there is no foolproof method, or combination of methods, which work 100% of the time for 100% of the people. Therefore every small factor and broker needs to discover which methods work best for them. But how?

Several contributors answered this in unison: you must use marketing methods that best suit your personality, skills, and interests, and you must use them constantly. Marketing, if you will, becomes a way of life. Marketing is not separate from the rest of your business, unconnected to anything else you do. Marketing encompasses all your activities and everything your business is.

In this regard, integrity, fairness, caring for clients, and providing exceptional service all attract people to your business. Solid, good business practices simply make your company desirable, and thereby are an extension of marketing.

While some marketing methods may move you outside your comfort zone (which isn't necessarily bad), if a particular method is too far outside, let's be honest: you're not going to try it. That's okay. Therefore, to determine which methods *you* should use, do a self-assessment of activities you enjoy and skills you have. When you have knack for anything – computer technology, public speaking, writing, whatever – marketing methods that utilize your unique skills will work best for you.

Figuring out how to market effectively is not easy, and many don't have instant success as they start. However, this book has shown what marketing methods work (and don't work) for our eight contributors in the trenches. They have generously shared their experiences and given many sage pieces of advice. You are free to – indeed, you *must* – fashion your own unique marketing program, learning from these experiences and suggestions.

You may need to learn some particulars as to how to best use these methods for a small factoring business. But once you do, your marketing will be both enjoyable and effective, and bring in steady business for a long time to come. When you *do* find methods that are highly effective, perfect them and *work* them. Over and over again. But don't get complacent. The world is ever-changing, and honing your marketing skills (and learning new ones as time and technology produce them) is a never-ending exercise.

In closing, I join the contributors to this book in wishing you the very best in your business. As you bring the powerful financial tool called factoring to clients who will benefit from its use, may they – and you – profit richly from your efforts!

Appendix

Contributors' Information

Contributor	Company	Website	Location
Kim Deveney	American Funding Solutions LLC	www.funding4you.com	Blue Springs, MO
Melissa Donald	LDI Growth Partners	www.ldifactors.com	Walnut Creek, CA
Ryan Jaskiewicz	12five Capital, LLC	www.12five.com	Oakbrook Terrace, IL
Tony Neglia	Stonebridge Financial Services, Inc.	www.stonebridgefs.com	Brentwood, TN
Anne Gordon	Guilin Group, Inc.	www.guilinfunding.com	Wickford, RI
RaeLynn Schkade	Integrity Factoring	www.integrityfactoring.com	Grandview, ID
Don D'Ambrosio	Oxygen Funding, Inc.	www.OxygenFunding.com	Lake Forest, CA
Jeff Callender	Dash Point Financial Services, Inc.	www.DashPointFinancial.com	Tacoma, WA

Books and Ebooks
The Small Factor Series

Book 1
*Factoring Wisdom:
A Preview of
Buying Receivables*
Short Sayings and Straight Talk
For New & Small Factors

Book 2
*Fundamentals
for Factors*
How You Can Make
Large Returns in Small Receivables

Book 3
*How to Run
a Small Factoring Business*
Make Money in Little Deals
the Big Guys Brush Off

Book 4
*Factoring Case Studies
(2nd Edition)*
Essential Lessons from
30 Real Factoring Clients

Book 5
*Marketing Methods
for Small Factors
and Brokers*
Tools from the Trenches
To Make Your Factoring Business
Thrive!

About This Series

The Small Factor Series is designed to:

1. Provide a succinct introduction and summary of the books in this series as well as other writings by Jeff Callender.

2. Introduce readers to the investment of factoring small business receivables.

3. Provide a step-by-step manual with complete instructions for small factors.

4. Provide 30 real-life examples of factoring clients from the files of people who have been investing in small receivables for some time.

5. Describe and analyze numerous marketing methods to bring in new business which have been used by the eight contributors to the book.

Each book in the series is written to address the above points:

- Book 1, *Factoring Wisdom: A Preview of Buying Receivables,* introduces and summarizes the other books with brief excerpts from each, and arranges them by subject matter.

- Book 2, *Fundamentals for Factors* introduces potential factors to the business.

- Book 3, *How to Run a Small Factoring Business,* is the step-by-step manual.

- Book 4, *Factoring Case Studies* (2nd Edition), describes experiences of 30 real clients of small factors, which illustrate the many lessons and suggestions made in Books 2 and 3.

- Book 5, *Marketing Methods for Small Factors & Brokers*, includes contributions from seven small factors and an experienced broker.

Other Books by Jeff Callender

Factoring:
Sell Your Invoices Today,
Get Cash Tomorrow

How to Obtain Unlimited Funds without a Loan

Written to introduce factoring to small business owners, this book compares factoring to traditional lending, shows how it can help a company's cash flow, and guides readers in determining if factoring can improve their business.

The above books are available in the following formats from DashPointPublishing.com:
- Paperback
- PDF
- Kindle
- iPad & Android

Ebooks by Jeff Callender

Accounting Methods for Factors and Their Clients

By Robert Vasquez and Jeff Callender

This ebook describes how to establish and maintain proper bookkeeping records for a factoring company and factoring clients. You'll learn how to use GAAP-approved procedures and make sure you're doing it right. Following these step-by-step instructions starts you on the right foot.

How I Run My One-Person Factoring Business

Want to get started running a small factoring business by yourself? This ebook shows how the author successfully began as a one-person operation, and the everyday tools you can use now to do the same.

How I Run My Virtual Factoring Office

A virtual office means you can work from just about anywhere you want. Learn the common tools and technology the author uses (available to anyone) to run his virtual factoring office. Enjoy the comforts of home – at work!

"Top 10" Ebooks by Jeff Callender
"Top 10" Ebooks for Factors:

Top 10 Insights about Factoring Prospects

Questions to Ask
and Truisms to Remember
When Considering Potential Clients

Top 10 Illusions about Risk and Loss

Faulty Assumptions for
Factors and Brokers to Avoid

Top 10 Statements You Never Want to Hear

Unwelcome Words for Factors
From or About Their Clients

10 Key Points to Look for in Factoring Software

Consider these 10 issues
before purchasing software
for your factoring operation

"Top 10" Ebooks for Clients:

***Top 10 Quotes
on the Benefits of Factoring***

Statements from Business Owners
Who Factor Their Receivables

***Top 10 Misconceptions
about Factoring***

Assumptions and Perceptions
That Just Aren't True

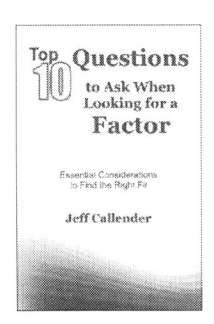

***Top 10 Questions to Ask
When Looking for a Factor***

Essential Considerations
to Find the Right Fit

The above ebooks are available in the following formats from DashPointPublishing.com:
- PDF
- Kindle
- iPad & Android

Acknowledgments

I would like to thank the following people for the important parts they played in creating this book:

The **contributing writers** who generously gave their time, experiences, wisdom, and insights. Without them this book could not have been written.

Nicole Jones for her proofreading skills and creating the ebook versions of books in the Small Factor Series and all other titles, and making them available to the world.

Anne Gordon for her proofreading skills and valuable experience, comments and support.

Cover image credit: © Imagehit International Ltd/123RF.com

Important Notice

This publication is for educational purposes only and is not intended to give legal, tax, or professional advice. If such service is needed, the reader should seek professional advice from a competent attorney or accountant.

The author and publisher assume no responsibility for any financial losses a reader may experience as a result of any factoring or other business or investment transaction.

Also by Jeff Callender

Paperbacks and Ebooks
The Small Factor Series includes 5 titles:
1. *Factoring Wisdom: A Preview of Buying Receivables*
   Short Sayings and Straight Talk for New & Small Factors © 2012
2. *Fundamentals for Factors*
   How You Can Make Large Returns in Small Receivables © 2012
3. *How to Run a Small Factoring Business*
   Make Money in Little Deals the Big Guys Brush Off © 2012
4. *Factoring Case Studies*
   Essential Lessons from 30 Real Factoring Clients
                   1st edition ©2003, 2005; 2nd edition © 2012
5. *Marketing Methods for Small Factors & Brokers*
   Tools from the Trenches to Make Your Factoring Business Thrive!
                                                           © 2012

Factoring: Sell Your Invoices Today, Get Cash Tomorrow
   How to Obtain Unlimited Funds without a Loan © 2012

eBooks
For Factoring Clients:
Accounting Methods for Factors & Their Clients © 2012
Top 10 Quotes on the Benefits of Factoring © 2012
Top 10 Misconceptions about Factoring © 2012
Top 10 Questions to Ask When Looking for a Factor © 2012

For Factors:
Accounting Methods for Factors & Their Clients © 2012
How I Run My One-Person Factoring Business © 2008, 2012
How I Run My Virtual Factoring Office © 2012
Top 10 Insights about Factoring Prospects © 2008, 2012
Top 10 Illusions about Risk and Loss © 2008, 2012
Top 10 Statements You Never Want to Hear © 2008, 2012
10 Key Points to Look for in Factoring Software © 2008, 2012

Spreadsheet Calculators
APR and Income Calculators © 2002, 2012

Software
FactorFox Software © 2006 – current year

Websites
www.DashPointPublishing.com   www.SmallFactor.com
www.DashPointFinancial.com   www.SmallFactorAcademy.com
www.FactorFox.com   www.FactorFind.com

About the Author

Jeff Callender had an unusual start to his business career. Though he is the son and grandson of businessmen, he began his working life as a pastor.

After earning a college degree in Sociology and a Master of Divinity degree, he served three churches in Washington state over 14 years. While he found ministry rewarding, he realized he had an entrepreneurial spirit which gradually pulled him toward business.

He left his career in the church and about a year later stumbled onto factoring. He began as a broker but after numerous referrals were declined only because of their small size, he started factoring very small clients himself. His career as a factor – and as a pioneer in the niche of very small receivables factoring – was thus born in 1994.

He has worked with a great number of very small business owners in need of factoring. He wrote his first book, *Factoring Small Receivables*, in 1995, and since then has written numerous books, ebooks, and articles, and spoken at many events in the factoring industry. His writing and two decades of experience have established him as a leading authority in the niche of small business factoring.

Jeff is the President of three companies he started. Dash Point Financial provides factoring services to small business owners throughout the U.S. It also provides the nucleus of his experience for writing. Learn more at DashPointFinancial.com.

Dash Point Publishing publishes and sells his books and ebooks, as well as those of other authors who write about factoring. His paperbacks are available from DashPointPublishing.com, as well as Amazon, the Kindle bookstore, Apple's iBookstore, and other online ebook sellers. Dash Point Publishing's website provides additional materials such as legal documents for smaller factoring companies.

FactorFox Software offers a cloud-based database solution for factors to track their client transactions. Originally based on his own company's back-office operational needs, readers of his books will feel right at home using the software in their own factoring companies. It has become one of the top platforms for the industry and is used by factoring companies throughout the world. More information can be found at FactorFox.com.

Having grown up in southern California, Jeff now lives in Tacoma, Washington with his wife, dog, and two cats. He has a grown son and daughter.

Made in the USA
Lexington, KY
26 November 2013